Tales of a Tenacious Tenor

Robert P Mitchell

TALES OF A TENACIOUS TENOR
Written by Robert P Mitchell
Copyright © 2013 by Robert P. Mitchell

Editing by Carrie Snider
Cover Art by Diogo Lando

ISBN: **978-0992396381**

First Published 2013 by ASJ Publishing

www.asjpublishing.com

10 9 8 7 6 5 4 3 2 1

DEDICATION

To all those that asked,
"Why aren't you singing at the Met?"

TABLE OF CONTENTS

Prologue How It All Started—Mario Lanza   1

Chapter 1 High School—Early Training   4

Chapter 2 College Years—Mansfield STC   17

Chapter 3 Ocean Grove—The Life Changing Summer   26

Chapter 4 The Long Climb Begins—Mannes College Of Music   38

Chapter 5 Where Do We Go From Here? Spear Carrying A City Opera   62

Entr'acte   69

Chapter 6 Metropolitan Opera Council Auditions   70

Chapter 7 A Trip to Germany   79

Chapter 8 Aspen, and Then   87

Chapter 9 Performing at Last   89

Chapter 10 A Banner Year   95

Chapter 11 Rodolfo, Middlesex, Opera Studio   104

Chapter 12 The Next Decade to Opera Classics   111

Chapter 13 Regina Opera – Pagliacci   128

Regina Opera - Norma   133

Chapter 14 A Big Name Voice Teacher   140

Chapter 15 How Do We Go On From Here   146

Epilogue Aftermath   152

Opera Repertoire   154

Amato Opera Company Repertoire   156

Author Acknowledgements   158

Photo Credits   159

About The Author   164

(Credit Konstanin Moskalenko for all bxw Amato performance photos).
Robert Mitchell as Radames in Verdi's *AIDA*, Act 4, Scene 1

Opera? Ya mean like Pavaroddy?
Yeah-h… Somp'm like 'at.

Prologue

How It All Started—Mario Lanza

July, 1954

As I was about to run out the back door of the kitchen, Mom called to me.

"Happy birthday, Robert!"

They didn't call her "Cricket" for nothing, a name she loved. Maybe she was small of stature, but she could stand tall when she needed to. Like the time she chased my older brother Johnny and me up the narrow back steps with a hefty dust pan brush, whacking us on the behind, or on whatever part she could reach. Like crickets, Mom could make a lot of noise. That's why we kids used to let her take on Dad for us. But this morning I hardly noticed behind her apron that she was wearing loose-fitting slacks and a brown blouse, not her usual kitchen attire. The blouse complemented her brown eyes—all us Mitchells had brown eyes and brown hair. Her hair was neatly pinned back without her usual bandana.

I stopped, turned, pulled out the sides of my blue checkered swimming trunks, and bowed gallantly to her. "Thanks, Mom. Hey! I'm fifteen today and I'm going swimming at Hanna Park!"

"But Dad's showing movies over in Bellefonte." It was the fifteenth of July, all right, and she must have already decided she was taking me to the movies today.

"Not today, Mom. It's too nice out. My buddies 'll be there." This day brightened my spirits in this muggy, sweltering summer in Lock Haven, Pennsylvania.

From our house at 83 Susquehanna Avenue, Bellefonte was a forty-five minute trip.

"Oh, I forgot. Dad's showing the *Black Lagoon* today, isn't he?" Remembering that Dad was showing a new horror film all my friends wanted to see, I suddenly realized I would be the first to see it, so I changed my mind and quickly replied, "Okay, I'll go."

Before she could stop me to explain what she had in mind, I bounded up the stairs three at a time to change into my denim shorts and my old red T-shirt. By the time I came back down, Mom had shed her trusty apron and was already waiting behind the steering wheel of the old, family Plymouth.

As we drove up the "Altoona Road" (State Route 2022) Mom said rather sullenly, "I'm not taking you to a horror picture." She turned to me with a big smile, "Do you know what's playing in the other theater in Bellefonte?"

I had no idea, but I knew the "other" theater was the fancy one in town. When his printing business was slow, Dad worked occasionally at the "second" theater Johnny and I called the "ratty" one, with seats like in school auditoriums, the popcorn and candy came from a vending machine, no ushers, and the bathrooms stank. But they showed the movies we liked.

Without waiting for me to reply she added, "The Student Prince."

I looked at her and started to say, "The what?" but immediately realized it was the latest Mario Lanza movie. Actually, I did want to see it, but at the moment I wasn't in the mood for a romantic love story. I wanted the thrill of a monster in a black lagoon chasing pretty girls around, and to laugh at the hero's side kick. "I don't want to watch a sappy love story," I replied and looked out my window. After all, it's MY birthday today, I thought to myself.

"But Robert, you said you couldn't wait to hear Mario sing again," she cooed, while nudging me in the ribs. She knew he was my singing idol, and gave me that oh-come-on-now-Robert-you-know-you-want-to-see-it look, a look that always worked on Dad. I liked to pretend it didn't sway me, but I caved in much quicker than I ever thought I would.

"Oh-h…all right, Mom… But this better be good!"

From the first song, "Summertime in Heidelberg," I was hooked. As the love story began to unfold, I hunched down in my seat so Mom couldn't see the tears streaming down my face. If she told Johnny and our two sisters how gushy I was, I'd be dead meat. Kathie, the barmaid, was played by the most beautiful woman I had ever seen, Ann Blythe. When she was on screen I couldn't take my eyes off her. When she and Mario sang together, oh how I wanted to be in his shoes!

Mom never said a word about my fidgeting: running my hands through my hair, looking away from the screen, using the crook of my elbow to dry my cheeks. But she knew. Mothers always do.

When we walked out of the theater, she smiled, but didn't say a word. I was lost in my own adolescent romantic fantasies, not to mention Mario's voice still ringing in my ears. As we walked across the parking lot to the car, I fell back of her a little so she couldn't see my tear-stained face and red-puffed eyes. Most of the ride home, I looked out the window as the wind whistled by. At first we didn't talk, but then, she broke the silence.

"What did you think of his voice?" she asked, trying not to notice my puffy eyes.

Still looking out of the window trying to un-puff my eyes in the breeze, I said without looking at her, "Terrific! ... I never heard him on a big screen like that before." I peeked at her reflection in the windshield to try to measure where this conversation was headed.

"Wouldn't you like to sing like that?"

Abruptly I turned toward her, blew through my lips, and whispered, "Are you kidding?"

She smiled that familiar Mona Lisa smile and then looked straight ahead. "Just keep at it, that's all."

I stared at her for a moment and then looked out the window again, shaking my head. Mom, the eternal wishful thinker. Meanwhile my emotions bounced back and forth like a billiard ball, from I can do this! to, No I can't! Dad's favorite prediction resounded in my head: You'll never amount to a tinker's damn! But Mom had unknowingly fueled a fire in me.

Sensing my delicate mood, she tried to distract me from my thoughts with idle chatter the rest of the ride home. That evening after supper, while they were watching TV in the living room, I came down the back stairs and tip-toed out the kitchen door to the backyard—I needed to be alone for a while. As a child my prayers were pretty much rote, like, "Now I lay me down to sleep...," but this night my heart was bursting. Tears streamed uncontrollably down my cheeks. I looked up at the star-glistened sky, trying to frame a prayer with my arms raised to God. No words came to me. Suddenly my passion took over, and out loud my soul raised my innermost thoughts to God for me.

"Dear God, I wanna sing ... I gotta sing, like that, like Mario ... Please, God ... help me!"

Chapter 1
High School—Early Training

1939 - 1957

We Mitchells were a singing family. We sang in church, in school and at home and on holidays. Mom would sit at the piano and call, "Com'on you guys. It's Christmas. Time to sing."

With glad smiles, we'd gather around and sing to her accompaniment, be it Christmas carols, Easter hymns, Thanksgiving songs, whatever the holiday. We each had our own part to sing. My two elder sisters, Joan and Margaret ("Cissy") sang alto, Mom sang soprano, my brother, Johnny, sang tenor, and Dad and I—the baby of the family—sang bass and baritone respectively.

"Hey, Mom, let's sing "Winter Wonderland," I would suggest at Christmas.

"I can't play that one," Mom would say with a sly smile that said, "Now Robert, you know better than to ask for something I can't play."

"How about, 'Silent Night?'"

"Now you're cookin'."

We certainly didn't compare with the Trapp Family Singers, but we made a reasonably good sound, but more importantly, it brought us together as a family.

My parents were polar opposites. Mom provided the cheery atmosphere in the household with her sense of humor and music. She had a mischievous streak and loved to laugh. As she hung the laundry or swept the floors she sang, usually old Gospel tunes she grew up with. Dad, on the other hand, was all business. The print shop and making money consumed him. But even he at holiday time could be persuaded to join in. His favorite song was an old Gospel hymn, "Ivory Palaces," which he could plunk out on the piano with his index finger—that and "Carolina Moon." Mom could get a smile out of him better than anyone by encouraging him to sing. But he could never let his hair down because he carried the weight of the world on his shoulders, worrying about money and how to feed his family. He seemed to get really uptight around Christmas when business was slow. Other times when business picked up, he could be downright jolly.

That was especially true in the summertime. Mom would walk into the room and say, "Anybody for a picnic?" our favorite family pastime—besides singing.

"Yeah, yeah! Where to?" we kids would yell.

Dad would say, "Just a minute! Let me finish this job...."

He loved to drive us to all the parks in central Pennsylvania for a cookout. His passion was grilling burgers while Johnny and I played cowboys and Indians in the woods. I really don't know what Joan and Cissy did all that while. We waited for his "Come and get it before I throw it all out," before we'd run out of the woods to gobble down some picnic chow. Then we were right back in the woods to resume our games.

Joan, the eldest of us kids, took after Mom with her perky sense of humor and good cheer. When our neighbor, Sammy Smith picked on me, Joan would run out of the house and yell, "You leave my brother alone, Sammy Smith." If he persisted, she'd tackle him and hold him down until I got away. Sammy was twice my size, but not Joan. She was his age and a tomboy who later majored in physical education. He was no match for her. I never thanked her for her sisterly devotion to me.

Cis was the serious one, very studious and a really good student. Johnny wasn't dumb by any means, but he was always getting himself into trouble in school, and his grades showed it.

Like Cis, I was serious and very conscientious. I always had good grades. When I brought a report card home, Mom eyed it for anything that wasn't an A (=excellent).

"What did David get?" was her usual question. My best friend, David Wolfe, excelled in all subjects (except gym), and he was her measuring rod for my success. If she saw a B, she would say, "Why didn't you get a A? What did David get?"

"I don't know what David got, Mom, but he probably did get an A." If she pursued the issue, I soon learned to deflect her. "Hey, Mom! I got a solo in chorus this week. Maybe I can sing it in church." That usually did the trick, so I didn't have to stand there and defend myself about my grades. I always did the best I could, and that should have been enough. But it never was.

Mom always used to say about my desire to sing: Just keep at it. At what? To sing like Mario I needed singing lessons. She hadn't a clue. And Dad? All he cared about was "the business" he wanted me to take over some day. Did I care about that? Well, sometimes I did think seriously about it, and it wasn't just to please him, but when I tried to discuss it with him, what happened? We ended up fighting about it.

He would yell at me that I was too green to tell him anything about business, and I'd counter that maybe he should try living in the twentieth century for a change, instead of in the ancient printing guilds.

"What's wrong with the guild system?" he would roar.

I'd start to walk away. What was the use of telling him there's nothing wrong with the guilds? That wasn't the point. We just happened to live in the twentieth century, not the fourteenth. Maybe we could have discussed how to bring the business into the twentieth century…?

"There you go spending my money again!" he would shout. "We can't afford…!"

Here we go again about the money. I think every conversation I ever had with my dad went round in circles and ended with money talk. We just couldn't get on the same page. I would go upstairs to my room or take a ride on my bike to try to clear my head.

If only I could sing like Lanza, every girl would throw herself at my feet. Singing's my ticket to feeling good about myself, and a good future. But how can I get started…?

Then Dad learned I was serious about becoming a singer.

Dad had a tough life. His father died when he was about thirteen or so, and Grandma raised him by herself. He had a nervous breakdown of some sort, and they wouldn't take him in the army—at least that's how I understand it. I saw in youthful pictures that he was thin and quite handsome with his Clark Gable moustache and full head of hair. But I guess everything he tried didn't work out for him, so he became a very bitter man. He had become rather heavy, his face deeply lined and rather pasty. But he still had a full head of hair, and not a single grey one.

"You and your goddamn pipe dreams! You'll never amount to a damn thing! Get a real job! You'll never do what you want to do, anyhow. You'll do what you have to do. That's life! You'd be better off in the Army! They'll kick some sense into you."

That August I worked for Dad setting type in his print shop. He had bought two new presses and installed them in what used to be the dining room—it faced the side street, accessible for deliveries. He had taught me how to set type, a "modern" eighteenth century technique. While I set type he ran the presses. We listened to the radio while we worked, programs like Arthur Godfrey Time, a morning variety show. We enjoyed the singing, the antics, and laughed together.

Dad could be a caring teacher one minute, and a roaring lion the next. He loved to lecture, or what I called "pontificate" about money (making a living), politics and religion. I guess my problem was that I never learned Mom's trick: just let him ramble until he runs out of steam. Instead, I argued with him. At first he loved my jabs so he could further expand on his ideas. But if you showed him how he was wrong when he really was, he'd go ballistic.

There was an evening after supper as we worked in the shop, he was holding forth about religion. Suddenly I remembered I had a rehearsal with Mrs. Kamp, the church organist. I got up and removed my apron. Immediately Dad yelled at me, "Wait a minute! I'm still talking to you. Where the hell do you think you're going?"

"I have a rehearsal with Mrs. Kamp."

"What rehearsal? I've got to get these funeral cards out for Johnny Yost tonight. Did you finish setting them up?"

"Ah, no, Dad."

He slammed down the type he was installing in the printer and turned to me with a face like a banshee, "Goddamn it, Robert! I told you before we have to get them done toni-…"

Continuing to face the type case where I'd been working, I cut him off. "Dad, I can't let Mrs. Kamp down." Swinging my chair around to him, I continued, "I'll do it in the morn-…"

"To hell with Mrs. Kamp!" stamping his foot on the floor. "Don't you know what's important in life? She can find anybody to sing her … music." Now shaking his hands in the air, "How're you ever gonna amount to anything in life if you keep running after that fool's errand you call 'singin'?' You'll be scrubbin' floors all your life!" His face burned scarlet.

By this time I felt my face burning like his, and my chest tighten, so I turned to him face to face and shouted back, "You don't even pay me for this lousy job!" and turned on my heel and rushed out of the room as I angrily threw my apron over the type case.

When I got outside, there was Mom waiting in the car to drive me to church. It was already getting dark. She could see in my face that something was wrong. Before she asked I told her about the fight we had just had and how I walked out on him.

She sighed in exasperation. Her face paled, even in the dark. I guess she knew she was in for it with Dad, and she would have to run interference for me, as she has done for all of us kids throughout their married life. Mom was the family peacemaker, a role she took on herself, but I don't think she liked it very much.

"That wasn't very nice," she commented, meaning me, I think. I couldn't be sure whether she was on his side or mine. The fact that she was ready to drive me to church I thought meant she was on my side. But Mom was afraid of Dad, so perhaps I had put her in a bad position. I guess she knew about my rehearsal, but didn't know Dad expected me to work that night.

"What am I supposed to do, Mom?" shaking my hands imploringly toward her. "He doesn't give a damn about me."

She shook her head. "Daddy loves you. He's grooming you to take over the business someday."

"Yeah, like he groomed Joan, and tried with Cissy and Johnny, right? That leaves me, the last of his progeny. What if I don't want the stupid business? Besides, I can't work with him. He drives me nuts. What about my music? My singing? I thought you liked my singing."

"You can always do that on the side."

What? I thought you wanted me to sing…

Mom's support of my singing was always a bit schizophrenic. Singing in church and school was fine. And she loved the idea that I wanted to sing like Mario. Yet when I got serious about a career, she clammed up. She knew Dad didn't like the idea, so she probably felt she was in the middle. I didn't know. She wouldn't talk about it. I always wanted to scream, but could only sputter. My thoughts became so jumbled all I could do was shut myself down.

This night I had no retort for her. The drive to church felt like being in Johnny Yost's funeral hearse. Mom waited for me in the car. She didn't even come in to hear me sing.

On the way home we talked about the ups and downs of Mrs. Kamp's health. She's in her eighties, after all, I kept thinking to myself. But I loved that lady and felt guilty for thinking like that. Is Mom in my camp or not? Is there anyone who'll support and help me?

In my lone hours for the remainder of that summer of '54, whether in my room or in the woods, I talked to God, agonizing over and over what

I should do. God, why shouldn't I believe in my dream? Waiting for God takes patience, never my strong suit. I may as well wait for Godot. Sometimes I was feeling up, sometimes down, while other times everyday pressures gobbled my attention. Before I knew it, the summer had ebbed away.

In September after school started, I had no time for the print shop. As I rode my bike from school to my new paying job at the drugstore, I decided I had to prove Dad was wrong. But, by the time I got to my post behind the tobacco counter, I again had second thoughts about singing.

If I can't learn to sing like Mario, how can I prove the Old Man wrong?

I knew I had to come up with a plan to learn how to sing—properly.

As I grew older, choir directors always put me in the baritone section. But the more I learned about music, playing in the band and later studying the piano, the more I felt something was amiss about my voice: I couldn't sing the lower notes. That was when I started to think I was really in fact a tenor. And Johnny sang tenor, so, whatever he did I wanted to do. He was my big brother, after all.

I turned to Mrs. Graves, the choral teacher in high school, the only person I knew who taught singing. She offered to give me lessons for free, not because she believed in me, but that she saw how much I wanted to sing.

During one lesson she said, "Bob, I know how much you want to sing, but you should think of singing as a second career, an avocation, not a vocation. You can find all sorts of venues where people will enjoy hearing you. But as a career? There are too many struggling artists out there looking to make careers. Your chances are slim, believe me." She shook her head decisively with her lips pressed together.

I wanted to say to her, "But Mrs. Graves, I at least want to try. What's the harm in that?" But I kept my peace and went away more discouraged than ever. "Nobody cares what I want," I whispered to no one in particular as I slunk down the hall.

Summer, 1955

Up to this point I thought of singing in terms of Mario. To me, opera singers were large women with horns on their heads brandishing spears in one hand and large shields in the other. Or maybe a fat little man decked out in a tuxedo, squeezing out his high notes. Lanza was different. He's what I wanted to be.

My introduction to opera came from across Susquehanna Avenue where the Fontana family lived. Mr. Fontana was an amateur opera singer, quite well known in Lock Haven. The Mitchell family didn't know about such things; we didn't move in those circles. I had no idea Mr. Fontana was an opera singer until Johnny told me so. In fact, Johnny was taking lessons with Mr. Fontana. I decided to check Mr. Fontana out for myself.

If you saw him on the street, you'd never take Mr. Fontana for an opera singer. He worked as a signal repairman for the Pennsylvania Railroad, always in his dirty, oil-stained, blue-denim overalls. He was a tall man with a ruddy, yet dark outdoor complexion, unruly salt and pepper hair, topped with a striped railroad hat that must have been handed down from a nineteenth century predecessor. His hands were large and strong and perpetually black from fixing greasy railroad signals, I guessed. He wore thick glasses, giving him the curious appearance of a professor who'd taken a wrong turn.

I was excited the day I was to talk to him about singing. Maybe he could help me learn to sing like Mario and launch me into a fabulous singing career. My imagination soared as I crossed Susquehanna Avenue, imagining myself in a dashing costume, brandishing a sword at some foe, singing for the hand of Ann Blythe, who soon joined me in a romantic duet.

My dream abruptly vaporized as I stepped across the well-worn threshold of the Fontana front door. The reality of smoky, acrid air tickling my nose and burning my throat shook me right out of my reverie. My eyes burned as though I had just walked into a forest fire. It came from the wood burning stove in the kitchen, which was Mrs. Fontana's well-guarded domain.

What did they burn in there? Old, worn-out boots?

As my eyes adjusted to the dark room, shadows of old country house and well-used furniture crowding the room began to take shape before me. My eyes swept round the room, wondering if anyone was home.

An upright piano stood against the wall to my left on the far side of the door to the kitchen. Mr. Fontana, tools dangling from an elaborate tool belt, sat rather agitatedly on the piano bench facing the door waiting for me as planned. Noticing him, I smiled and was about to say hello.

Before I could speak, without a word, he abruptly stood, tools clunking against the piano with resounding reverberations through the piano's sound board. He grabbed his cap with his right hand, fingers automatically finding their previously grease-smudged marks on the small visor, and as he turned toward the piano, he slapped the hat down on top of it and motioned me forward with his left hand, by this time, his back to me.

"Oh, thank you, Mr. Fontana, for seeing me today. You can't imagine how much I want to become a tenor..."

"You want to be a tenor? Have you ever sung tenor?"

I slowly shook my head.

"If you want to be a tenor you have to be able to sing this," he said, pointing to music on the piano rack. He opened to the page that would be my test and ordered me to sing the line of music indicated by a disturbingly greasy index finger.

What's this? I wondered to myself.

He switched hands and began thumping the notes on the piano with that same right hand index finger as he pointed to the Italian words in the score with a similarly black-stained left index finger, smudging the page as he did so. It was well worn and quite brown anyway, so he didn't even notice.

"Know Italian? ... No? Why not? You said you were a tenor. Well, sing any words you want," he bellowed in his stentorian baritone. "I want to hear your range."

Range?

I tried, but now tight as a hangman's noose, I could only squawk any notes I tried to sing."

"What?" he fumed. "You call yourself an opera singer?"

Wait a minute — I never said that.

Pointing to the front door he shouted, "Get out! You're not a tenor until you can sing this aria!" (Which, by the way, was "Oh, tu che in seno agli angeli," Alvaro's famous aria from Verdi's La Forza del Destino, an aria I did not look at until I was in my forties.)

He stomped out into the kitchen. I glanced around the corner of the kitchen door to see where he had gone, but the kitchen table held its ground and he had vanished. Not even Mrs. Fontana was there.

Turning back to the score on the piano, I looked quizzically at the notes and piteously pushed a couple of keys. I tried to sing the notes and wiped my fingertips on my pants, hoping Mom wouldn't notice any grease marks, shook my head, and, with my chin on my chest, shuffled forlornly out of his house and back across Susquehanna Avenue. I guess God was watching the traffic because I wasn't. It was a very long walk home.

For months after, I wondered, If this is opera, why bother? I can't do this. I turned my attention to other pursuits like practicing the piano, school work, my job at the drugstore, and church activities. For recreation I rode my bike—everywhere. I even tried to ride to Bellefonte one time, but turned back at Linda Miller's farm out on Eagle Valley Road beyond Mill Hall.

Still later, wondering if I really were a baritone as my teachers insisted, I decided to buy some recordings to test this hypothesis. I really had no idea how to obtain them. The music store downtown featured mostly pop music. Ordering through them was too expensive, I found out. Although I never went back to Mr. Fontana for lessons, Johnny and I had struck up a friendship with the youngest Fontana, named Joseph.

Joe was college-age, but he took some mysterious delight in deigning to have us listen to his phonograph records, of which he was immensely proud. Unlike his father, Joe wore no glasses and was light complexioned, but with very black hair, and though clean shaven, you could see the dark traces of a full black beard. He also had blue eyes, which didn't seem to fit the Fontana image, but then his sisters were also rather fair—like their mother, I presumed. Also unlike his father, Joe's girth demonstrated clearly that he led pretty much a sedentary life. I remember him always in patterned short-sleeved shirts, summer or winter, with dark slacks. He studied math or engineering in college, but I don't know where, nor what he did. With a perpetual aura of mystery hovering over him, the rap my sisters provided was that he never dated and rarely left the house when home from college.

Joe hated opera, he hated singing, he hated chamber music, he hated choral music... Actually, anything that was not a symphony was garbage as far as he was concerned. The Fontanas had always been something of an enigma to us, but Johnny and I were intrigued by Joe's emerging attention. Besides, we thought we could learn something about the symphonic literature of which we knew absolutely nothing.

Maybe it was by way of consolation for the stunt his father had pulled on me that Joe magnanimously decided to help me buy my first opera recordings. When I told him about that day with his father, he grimaced as if he had tasted something very sour. He shook his head. "Can't get 'em in Lock Haven," he complained, jumping over my story, right to the business at hand. He told me he got his LPs by mail order from Sam Goody in New York.

As he opened the catalogue he said, "I hate opera," as if he had never mentioned it before, and whisked past the opera pages. With his nose in the air, as if to avoid being contaminated by them, he went right to the order form and showed me how to order records. My first choices were aria recordings of George London and Cesare Siepi, both leading Metropolitan Opera bass-baritones at the time. Well, Siepi was a pure basso.

"I hate singers," Joe grumbled all the while.

"Why do you hate singers? What have they ever done to you?" I asked.

"I don't know. I just do."

"But your father sings opera."

"Yeah. I've had to listen to it—and him—all these years. My father only listens to opera. No wonder I hate it!" We all laughed.

When the recordings arrived a few weeks later, I ran them over to show to Joe. "You can't play those things here!" he commanded as he opened the front door part way.

"I know!" I laughed. "Just wanted to show them to you, and say thanks."

"Okay. You showed me. That's enough! Now get those rotten things out of here!"

I grinned broadly. "Thanks again, Joe. I really appreciate your help." As he closed the door—almost in my face—I could see the hint of a smile creeping across his face.

I've treasured those records all my life: still have them. They're probably worth quite a bit by now. The Cesare Siepi recording, with Verdi arias on one side and assorted pieces on the other, is on the old, green, Cetra label, a company later bought by Angel Records. The George London LP, all Mozart, is on London Records with Bruno Walter conducting.

As I listened to them those first few days, I knew then that I didn't sound anything like London or Siepi—or Robert Merrill, a Met baritone of whom I acquired a record on my own in Wagner's Music Shop downtown. The more I tried to sound like them, the more I realized something was terribly wrong. It didn't feel right; nor it did sound right to me.

Right after Johnny graduated from high school in 1955, he joined the Navy. One Christmas he came home with a recording of Jussi Björling's September 24, 1954 Carnegie Hall recital, which he left behind when he went back on duty. I "appropriated" it. (Squatter's rights.) He never asked for it back. I still have this one as well.

Björling was the Pavarotti of his time, from the forties until his untimely death in 1960. Years later, I remembered the announcement of his death as though it were yesterday. I was home just prior to going to New York for my first year at the Mannes College of Music. A beautiful afternoon, I was playing badminton in a neighbor's yard with neighborhood friends. Mom came over to tell me of Jussi's death. Absolutely stunned, like an automaton I handed my racket to my partner, and without a word, walked slowly back to my room, and once there, bawled like a baby. I played his record over and over, making myself cry all the more.

His voice made up for any artistic deficiencies. Like Pavarotti, he too was not a good actor. His artistry was in the unique sound of his voice, his musicality, his passion, all wrapped up in his effortless and perfect singing control. Like Pavarotti, he had a voice that you recognize on the first note, and he too had high notes to burn. In fact, when Pavarotti first hit the big time, critics would say things like, "At last! We now have a tenor to carry Bjorling's mantle. First Caruso, then Gigli, followed by Bjorling. Pavarotti's singing last night surely places him in this distinguished line…"

Jussi sang at the Metropolitan Opera and all over the world. His singing was so precise and musical, and his sound so different from Mario's, more disciplined, more musical, I knew I had to somehow get serious about singing lessons. But with whom? I didn't know any voice teachers. Singing is too serious and personal to let your fingers do the walking.

By my junior year in high school, my eldest sister Joan was married and Johnny had joined the Navy, so Cissy and I were the only ones left at home. She and I had never gotten on well, but since we now had to share a bathroom, we began to try to work things out. It's called "survival." She was studying to be an English teacher at Lock Haven State Teachers College, within walking distance of our house.

One day as I was practicing the piano in the living room, she burst in, scaring me half to death because I didn't hear her coming. She was excited about having joined the college band and was dying to tell me about her new instructor, Mr. Frederick Pfliegger.

"Robert!" she shouted. "Mr. Pfliegger's a tenor!"

The shock nearly jolted me off the piano bench. I hated being interrupted at the piano. My glare should have shriveled her on the spot. Undaunted, she plowed right on. "He's a tenor, Robert! Maybe Mr. Pfliegger could teach you to be a tenor. Do you want me to ask him?"

Now the question froze my bottom to the bench. When was the last time Cissy wanted to do something for me? What does she want? I slowly turned to her and asked tentatively, "You would you do that for me?"

She smiled and nodded enthusiastically.

I thought, "What a change from slamming her bedroom door in my face and ordering me to go downstairs to get to the bathroom. Could I help it if her room was the only way to get there from my room—other than going down the front stairs, walk all the way to the back stairs, and climb back up? What if I really had to go? And I did knock, damn it all."

Something different just happened. My temper melted. I looked at her as though she were a new person, and said with all the sincerity I could muster, "Thank you, Cis. I really appreciate that."

Suddenly it occurred to me that Cis really did understand. Well, I already knew she understood my desire to sing because she too loved to sing, albeit in choirs. And it was she who first introduced me to Mario's records. But did she care a hoot about my wanting to sing opera, for which she cared nothing? This spontaneous offer spoke volumes: I was genuinely moved by it. After that things began to improve between us.

Cis was true to her word, and very soon I had an appointment with Mr. Pfliegger. After hearing me sing he demonstrated what a tenor sounded like by singing the beginning of the famous Handel aria from Messiah, the "Every Valley" portion that has very difficult roulades—that is, lots of fast notes up and down. His voice was very different from Mario's. Every note he sang had the precision of a good instrumentalist, and I realized that I had much to learn about singing.

He took me on, but decided I was a baritone.

My sense about that today is that my voice was not as light as his, so he, like many teachers, thought to protect my voice by not having me sing into the higher tenor range. I now judge that a mistake, but at the time I had no way to evaluate his decision, so I went with it.

I was disappointed, but thought that if my voice would darken into a baritone as I got older, so what? God decides what you'll be in the womb—or before. So, "if I am to be a baritone," I thought, "I want to be a good one."

Whatever I was, Mr. Pfliegger taught me a lot of good things about singing, so I stayed with him until I went to Mansfield State Teachers College in the fall of 1958.

Chapter 2

College Years—Mansfield STC

December, 1958

My first opera onstage came my first year at Mansfield STC. By this time, with a few years of voice lessons under my belt, I thought I was pretty hot stuff. But my voice teacher at MSTC, Jack Wilcox, didn't agree.

Jack towered over me by at least a head. He reminded me of the movie actor-singer, Howard Keel. Handsomer than Keel, Jack was built like a linebacker, but had the grace of a dancer. His smile lit up a room, as did his sonorous voice. He always seemed to be in a good mood, and put pep in my step just to be in his presence. His trade mark, if we can call it that, was his hair: always flowing, always needing to be pushed back where it belonged. The girls were gaga over him. So were some of the boys.

But—he put me in the chorus in Act 2 of La Boheme, which was part of the annual fall Opera Workshop production of which Jack was the director. I wasn't happy.

"I hate singing chorus—to me it's demeaning."

"Too bad, kid. You have no stage experience and I need you there. And you need to learn from the bottom, like every other profession or trade. Besides, I'm giving you some solo lines."

I was severely ticked off with him for this humiliation, but I was afraid to say anything more for fear he'd kick me out of the workshop. So, I went ahead and learned my lines and music. Better than nothing.

La Boheme takes place on Christmas Eve in 1830s Paris, and it was extremely cold—something of a mini ice age at the time—so our costumes consisted of itchy wool trousers with brightly colored sweaters and scarves that wouldn't stay put.

I was an orange hawker in this scene. Before I reached the stage with its hot lights, I was sweating under all the sweltering clothes. Most everyone assumed my oranges were fake, but we couldn't find fake ones so we used real ones. The extra weight added to my discomfiture.

Opening night I marched onto the stage with my tray of oranges to the very sprightly orchestral (but in our case, piano) accompaniment singing, "Come buy my oranges!" My first operatic performance!

Meanwhile the stage was a hurly-burly of activity: Jack had kids running around the stage, a juggler, a magician, dancers, couples roaming around, some singing chorus, others not, and a number of other hawkers like me—although they had no lines, doing it for the valuable stage experience.

My great debut in opera seemed to last about as long as a drink of water. All that sweat and toil for a lousy three or four lines. Plus, nobody remembers you. You're just part of the scenery. As much as I hated being in the chorus, I loved every second of being onstage in front of those bright lights and audience, and singing my heart out. I couldn't see the audience because of the lights, just shadows and the reflection of glasses flashing here and there. I nevertheless was always aware of people out there. I could feel their presence, and could feel whether or not they liked the show. I knew I would not be noticed, but regardless of what I felt at that moment, it's the audience that makes or breaks a performance. Isn't that what the song, "There's No Business Like Show Business" is all about?

Yep. I was hooked.

Later in the spring, Jack tapped me to sing a small baritone role in scenes from Carmen for a road show he took to local schools. Going on the road had a different feel. It was sweaty work, too, even without those hot stage lights—we usually sang on gym floors for several grades at a time. You could see the audience better without the bright lights in your face. If they were with you it was good. But if they were bored or misbehaving—which was rare—that was a real downer.

I loved traveling, whether near or far. Being with like-minded singers, gabbing in the van, sharing our dreams, discussing the music, the staging, gossiping about the singers we liked or didn't like, and then piling out of the van searching for a place to change into our ersatz costumes and apply the limited makeup we used on the road, all this was a new adventure for me.

I loved all of it!

The following spring of 1958 I sang my first solo role, Father Abernathy, in the musical, Guys and Dolls. It felt good to be out there onstage to sing all by myself. Well, actually, I was singing to my onstage daughter. The song was "More I Cannot Wish You."

For the first time I discovered that singing is communicating, both with another character you cared about onstage, and with the audience as well. I became aware that the audience was listening to me as well as watching her reaction to me. I could feel that they were with us. They wanted us to succeed. They were cheering for us even in their silent rapture. And then I became aware that the song and its music spoke to me as well.

Music has its own language that goes directly to your soul, through your ears, your brain, and most certainly, your heart. Whether it's instrumental, like Rachmaninov's Second Piano Concerto, or with singing, as in the love scenes from La Boheme, music speaks to me as only the voice of God can. Something gelled inside me, whispering:

This is you, Robert. Welcome to your destiny…

But show music isn't opera. "You said you wanted to be an opera singer," said Dad in my head.

Oh, go away Dad, and let me enjoy this moment…please! You've got to start somewhere.

Fall, 1958

My lessons with Jack Wilcox progressed very well my second year at MSTC. One day I rushed into his studio all excited about just having listened to my record of Jussi Björling again.

"Jack! I'm sure I'm a tenor…"

"Not that again!" he groaned as he got up from the piano and walked toward me.

I stood before him imploringly. "You must hear that my voice doesn't even sound like a baritone. Besides, I can't sing baritone low notes."

He laughed, with that great flash of white teeth along with the sweep of his hand to push his hair back into place. "Yeah, but you can't sing the high notes in the tenor range, either. What makes you think you're a tenor, anyway?" He retreated to the piano, but instead of sitting, he propped his right arm across the top from the back of the piano and smiled back at me.

Opening my Messiah score as I approached the piano, I said, "Let me sing something for you. I've been working on Handel's Messiah, [the very tenor solo that Mr. Pfliegger had sung for me the day I met him]. Mrs.

Kamp has asked me to sing, 'Comfort ye – Every Valley' in church for Advent—if I can manage it. OK?"

A carefully trimmed eyebrow went up, but before he could say no I eagerly placed the open score on the piano rack. I pointed to the page, beckoning him with my winning-est smile to come around and play it for me.

"Bob, you know me and the piano. We don't get along." We both laughed. "All right, let's see what you can do with this." He came around the piano, sat down, and played the chord for the first entrance. I moved to my usual spot to his left.

"Co-o-o-m – fort ye." So far so good. The words are repeated, but much higher in the next phrase. "Co-o-o-m – for—" (Voice-crack!) I grimaced as I looked up to the ceiling as if to ask God for help. "Damn!"

Jack turned to me, and with a Cheshire cat grin and a backhanded slap to my gut, he announced triumphantly in his most glorious, stentorian bass-baritone voice,

"Kid, you'll never be a tenor in a million years!"

Damn! Damn! Damn! ... I slunk out of his studio. If he weren't so big I would have punched that I-told-you-so grin right off his face.

Apart from my frustrations with singing, I was a good student in all subjects, especially in theory and ear training, so I was invited to pledge Phi Mu Alpha, the national music fraternity, during the fall semester of 1958. We were subjected to some serious hazing, which in retrospect makes me wonder how my voice survived the brutal winter of '58-'59.

But it was worth it! Being a part of this fraternity of fellow musicians around the country has brought about meaningful and rewarding connections—and continued to do so.

Jack loved opera as well as show music. He had some chinks in his armor, too, that he made the mistake of telling me. He had a passion to sing Iago's famous monologue "Credo in un Dio crudel" in Act 2 of Verdi's Otello.

"Bob, I can't seem to get that damn high F#. I crap it every time."

Well, a-ha! I discovered the reason for his difficulty on the night of our acceptance into Phi Mu Alpha. The ceremonies took place in the major performing venue at MSTC, Straughn Auditorium. We initiates sat way up in the back of the balcony. Jack conducted the small orchestra from the pit, and at the same time sang an aria from Mozart's The Magic Flute—with Phi Mu Alpha words, of course. I was amazed to hear his rich voice ring all the way to the top of the auditorium with a radiance I had never heard before. The low F was spectacular.

At my next lesson I said, "Now I know why you can't get the high F#."

No smile this time. He stared at me from the piano bench, puzzled. I was in my usual spot.

"You're not a baritone at all," I said with my grandest smile.

"What? Are you going to tell me I'm a tenor now, too?" Ha, ha!

"No, no, of course not. You're not a baritone because you're a bass—a pure operatic basso."

"Get outta here!" He was smiling, but pushed me away affectionately.

"No, I mean it. You should have heard your low F from up in the balcony the other night. It was spectacular."

"Really?" Jack had a thoughtful, but doubtful look on his face.

Well, the upshot of the story was Jack was none too pleased. He thought of himself as a dramatic baritone, and my suggestion slid off like a kid down a wet slide. We never spoke of it again.

In high school I had ruined my father's rinky-dink violin, but Mr. Harold Brown, who conducted and taught the MSTC orchestra, convinced me to take up the instrument again. Mr. Brown, a diminutive man with unruly brown hair he habitually pushed back with his right hand, was a concert violinist himself, so he lent me one of his practice instruments, quite a generous gesture.

He shrugged it off, "You can't play without an instrument, can you?"

Like my father, Mr. Brown loved to give spur-of-the-moment lectures that rambled on and on. My friends always made fun of him, but I loved the man. Plus, he was so different from my father.

We shared a passion for the arts, philosophy, and the violin. He took me under his wing and began to look after me. One day in a lesson while we were working on bowing, he noticed my right elbow, deformed from playing backyard football.

"What happened to your elbow?" he asked as he took it in his hand like a doctor to examine it.

After my explanation he slapped himself on his forehead, a gesture that became all too familiar as I got to know him. He groaned. "My God, how could they have let this happen to you? Didn't they recognize your talent? Couldn't they have seen that you could have become an accomplished violinist? Why did they let you play football? It's a dangerous sport. Couldn't they see how talented you are? ..." and he went on and on complaining about the notorious "they" of my childhood.

Shaking his head sadly, he said, "If your right elbow had not been broken as a child, and if you had had the right teacher, and if you had dedicated yourself," pointing a finger in my direction, "there's no question whatsoever in my mind that you would have—and I say 'would,' not 'could,' you would have become a violin virtuoso. Look at your hands, your fingers," he said, taking each hand gently in his own and inspecting them as if they were sacred objects. "Your coordination, your superb musicianship," looking up into my eyes, "are absolutely perfect for the violin. No question about it." He paused, looked away, shaking his head gently, and then looked back at me with a sheepish smile, "But you want to sing..."

My eyes were so full of tears, I could only blink them down my cheeks as a response. He nodded his head, misinterpreting my tears by saying, "You're right—it is very sad. Not that you want to sing, but what they did to you, or rather, didn't do for you."

Actually my tears came from never having heard such a tribute in my life. No one had ever said anything to me even close to that. Being so used to criticism I felt unworthy of it, and yet I knew he meant what he said with all his being. I also knew that he had the expertise to offer such an amazing kudu. That made it still harder to take in.

At that time, I had no idea of his impressive musical background. He never mentioned that he had studied with luminaries such as Aaron Copeland and Nadia Boulanger. When I learned that, it made his words even more astounding.

Perhaps as a kind of recompense for the artistic ignorance shown me in childhood, Mr. Brown invited me to travel with him to New York City on weekends to sing with a group he founded, the Renaissance Chorus of New York. Even though it was a six-hour trip, I was thrilled because I wanted so much to become a part of the New York City music scene.

Although I was in awe of the Renaissance music we sang, I still didn't like singing in choruses. I felt I had to modify my voice, hold it back. At the same time, I was deeply moved by the intricate structures and fascinating harmonies the Renaissance composers had created. Plus, I learned much about early musical history, not to mention learning to sing complex ensemble music, sometimes as many as twelve or sixteen parts. Someday I would realize that these skills prepared me for difficult ensemble passages in opera, as well as enabling me to sing in professional choruses in New York.

Once on a return trip from New York one Sunday night, we ran into a severe snowstorm. I had a psychology test the following morning at eight o'clock with a professor I dreaded, and Mr. Brown did not want any criticism from the college administration about his driving me into New York on weekends.

At one point he swerved to miss a deer as the storm raged, and the car spun out of control off the road. For my safety he had insisted that I sit in the back seat (no seat belts in those days). When the car went out of control I grabbed both his and my violin and slid on top of them to the floor to protect them. When the car finally stopped we found ourselves in a ditch. Nobody was hurt, and the car was unscathed, but he nevertheless scolded me for thinking of the violins first—before my own safety.

No cell phones in those days, so Mr. Brown kept the car running to keep me warm while he went in search of help. It took hours to finally get us back on the road. We arrived back in Mansfield minutes before my class. Mr. Brown gave me pep pills to stay awake for the test.

They didn't work. I almost fell asleep during the test, but then they kicked in and I couldn't sleep for two days afterwards! I bombed the test, but managed to pass the course by writing a good paper.

* * * * *

I had never seen an opera in my life. So I asked a friend in the Renaissance Chorus to get me tickets for an opera at the Met. I said to him, "I don't care what the opera is. I just want to see an opera!"

It turned out to be Wagner's Tristan und Isolda, a very heavy opera for my first. But it also happened that Swedish soprano Birgit Nilsson made her much heralded Metropolitan Opera debut that night, December 18, 1959. I had never heard of her.

My seat was high in the second balcony near the back wall. A pillar—this was the old opera house on Thirty-Ninth Street—partially blocked my view of the stage, annoying me to no end. I noticed an empty seat in the first row as I sat down, only about two rows in front of me, and I kept eyeing it all through Act 1.

During the first intermission as people left their seats, I quickly made my way to that seat and sat down as if it were mine, neatly folding my coat on my lap as though I had just arrived. No one ever came to claim it, nor did my neighbors question my second act presence, so I enjoyed the rest of the opera from that great vantage point.

I'll never forget Nilsson's trumpet-like voice soaring through the house. After the "Liebestod" ("Love's Death") at the end of the opera, I thought I had died and gone to heaven with her. The ovation went on and on, but I had to get back to the apartment where I was a guest before they locked me out.

Little did I know that I had just witnessed the American debut of one of the greatest divas in operatic history as she began her world conquest.

* * * * *

My association with the young people in Mr. Brown's chorus was an early introduction to New York's Jewish culture. My new friends had names like Levin or Moshe or David or Naomi or Sarah or Rebekah. Hanging out with them seemed like coming home to me. The immediate identification I felt with them, which continued for years, became an impetus toward a lifelong interest in and study of Judaism. Never before had I met a group of people that loved opera and opera singers as they did. Their knowledge impressed me, so I eagerly soaked up their back-and-forth exchanges—to which I had little to add.

Mansfield's choruses also provided us with stimulating musical experiences, one being Karl Orff's Carmina Burana, another, Mozart's Requiem.

Carmina Burana is a fiendishly difficult piece, more so for young, inexperienced musicians. We spent the entire year learning it. Not only was the music hard, but we had to sing medieval German, French, and Latin. All this fed my knowledge of music, singing, history, and classical repertoire.

Mr. Hollenbach, the guest conductor, outraged all of us Mansfield students by bringing in soloists from the Eastman School of Music. We were not even allowed to audition.

I have to admit, none of us could have handled the difficult solo work in that piece. Certainly I could not have sung it at that time. In fact, I never sang it later, either.

Even though I was never an enthusiastic choral singer, later I came to appreciate and enjoy listening to good choruses. And, choral singing develops a sense of ensemble singing, a discipline necessary for singers, opera or otherwise.

* * * * *

In the spring of 1960, Jack mounted a full production of Most Happy Fella. I so badly wanted the role of Joey I would have killed for it. But, blast him! Jack gave it to his favorite voice student, a baritone he always favored over me. Angry and disappointed, I nevertheless took part in the show, growing somewhat accustomed to the disappointments of a singer's life in the theater.

Favoritism is a fact of artistic life, and one has to grow a tough skin for it. There's a saying in the arts, "It's not what you know, it's who you know." This is more the case than important people in theater will admit publically, but it's true, even down home. I've seen many a tear shed over a lost part, and even fine talent discouraged enough to stop singing or acting. It happened to me so often I look back and wonder how I stuck it out for as long as I did.

I had intended to finish my teaching degree at MSTC to become a teacher, but then came the exceptional summer of 1960 in Ocean Grove, New Jersey.

Chapter 3

Ocean Grove—The Life Changing Summer

Summer, 1960

The winter of 1959-1960 was tough. Getting back and forth the seventy or so miles from Lock Haven to Mansfield for occasional weekend breaks and holiday vacations in all that snow challenged even the snowplows. I usually commuted with an upper-classmate who had a tiny Nash Metropolitan that always got us through. Jan was a fearless driver. Nothing stopped her—she could have been a mailwoman. My memories of traveling with her seem limited to the brutal winter storms common to the Allegheny Mountains of north-central Pennsylvania. Her little two-seater Nash Metro had good tires and a trusty heater. When all else failed, when we couldn't see through the windshield in the blinding snow, or when the windshield wipers froze to the edge of the windows, that heater kept us toasty.

On one trip she asked, "How would you like to be a bellhop next summer down on the Jersey shore?"

At first I wondered, what's a bellhop? Then I zoned in on the Jersey shore part. "A job on the Jersey Shore? I've never been to the shore. I've never even seen an ocean. And earn money, too? You bet I'd love to go."

Jan explained that her uncle managed the North End Hotel on the boardwalk in Ocean Grove, New Jersey. She glanced over at me to see if I was listening—I was so quiet. "He's looking for young guys to be bellhops. It's a good job. You'll get lots of tips and it's not hard work. And there's the boardwalk and the beach right there…"

I just had to interrupt her, "How do I sign up?"

She put me in touch with her uncle and I got myself a summer job. I pictured myself running across a beach in my bare feet, diving into the surf. What a thrill: waves crashing ashore, pretty girls all over the place, beach, sunshine, and great restaurants! Things were looking up for me.

Until the next trip home from school.

As we sat in the kitchen drinking coffee, Dad was skeptical. With a scowl he asked, "How are you going to earn enough money for your tuition next fall? It costs money to live down at the shore."

I looked at him blankly. Of course I hadn't figured out all these details. I was still a kid! What do kids know? I glanced at Mom and nodded toward Dad. She picked up my cue: my Cricket softly entered the fray with her best cooing, soothing voice, "Now Ja-," Mom always cut off the last consonants of his name, "Robert says they'll give him room and board right in the hotel. Any money he makes is his. He should make plenty of tips in a place like that, right on the boardwalk. Don't you remember how Pop-pop loved Ocean Grove?" Pop-pop was Mom's dad.

Dad's scowl got worse.

"Well I'm not going to get stuck for any of your damned expenses, I've got enough of my own, keeping this family in house and home, so you'd better be damned sure you earn enough yourself."

And he marched back into the shop, coffee mug gripped so tight I thought it was going to squeal.

Mom and I looked at each other, I apprehensively. Slowly a smile curled the corners of her mouth upward. She looked at me with softer eyes than I had seen in a long time, "It'll be all right, Robert. You'll see."

The village of Ocean Grove featured the Great Auditorium, which was used for both religious and concert purposes. That summer they had hired opera singers as resident soloists for both sacred and secular music presentations. And they stayed at the North End Hotel. I recognized some of them from the posters around town as soon as they entered the hotel; others, from their voices as they spoke. One such singer was baritone Floyd Worthington.

From the moment he entered the lobby he had the aura of a celebrity. Although not quite as tall as I (five-nine), aside from his height he resembled Gary Cooper, with smooth light hair, tan fedora, long tan raincoat, the latter I suppose for style and just in case.

As he stood in front of the registration desk, people walked to and fro, buzzing about their luggage and getting to their rooms. His resonant voice caught my ear as his star quality captured my attention. I hastened over to him to pick up his large suitcase as he stood at the desk to register. The clerk then had little choice but to refer him to me. He turned towards me.

"Follow me, please, sir."

I led him to the elevator, and as I ushered him on, I told him I had him pegged as a singer because of his resonant, deep voice.

"Well, young man, you're quite right. I am indeed a singer." He reached into a satchel he carried under his arm and retrieved a small poster with his picture, taking up half the front page, dressed in a formal overcoat, white gloves, white scarf, topped by a dark fedora. He handed it

to me. "You may have this." (I still do.) On the front was a photo of him with these words

FLOYD WORTHINGTON
AMERICAN BARITONE
OPERA • CONCERT • RADIO-TV • ORATORIO •
MUSICALS • EUROPEAN TOURS 1960

On the back: a bio, another Gary-Cooper-look-alike picture, and reviews of concerts and operas he had sung with numerous regional companies.

He asked me if I was interested in singing. Flushing with pride I announced that someday I hoped to be up on stage with him.

He smiled graciously. "Really? That's wonderful! Where do you study?"

Trying to explain my variegated background would be as clear as pea soup, so I mentioned Mansfield STC. He knew of it, but was not familiar with its programs. At that moment the elevator stopped at his floor, so I picked up his suitcase and led him to his room. By the time we reached it he was holding forth about the dos and don'ts of making a career in singing. I listened intently. As I unlocked the door he asked if I were a tenor or a baritone. "I can't quite tell from your speaking voice," he observed.

"Well," I began hesitantly, "I think I'm a tenor, but my teachers tell me I'm a baritone."

"You should listen to your teachers. You could ruin your voice trying to sing out of your range," he said matter-of-factly as he looked for his room number.

"Here it is," I announced, walking ahead of him.

Once inside the room, he slipped off his coat and threw it across the nearest chair, and proceeded to demonstrate the proper way to breathe and produce a sound. He stood straight as a pole, yet relaxed, with his head held a little back, and quickly inhaled through his slightly open mouth. If I hadn't been watching intently I probably would have missed it.

He then began singing warm up scales. Soon he launched into an aria I didn't recognize. After singing the high note, he turned to me with a look that said, "What do you think?"

"Wow!" was all I could manage with a dropped jaw.

It was an impressive sound indeed. I thought the windows would crack and the people in adjoining rooms would begin to pound on the walls.

He didn't ask me to sing, so I asked him what I had to do to become a professional singer.

"Well," he started, but paused to sit down, "that's a difficult question to answer." He laced his hands together thoughtfully. Pointing to another chair, he added, "Sit down."

"Oh no, sir. I can't sit down on the job."

We both smiled. He acknowledged my comment with a dip of his head and continued.

"We all came into it in our own way. No two stories are alike."

"Do you need an agent," I began quickly, "or a manager, or someone like that? By the way, what does an agent do, and how is that different from a manager?"

"Whoa! One question at a time!"

"Sorry."

"It's okay," he continued. "This is a tough business. Have you read any bios of singers?"

I shook my head.

"Well, you should," he emphasized. "You'll get an idea from them. But—and this is a big but—bios are about the ones who became famous. That only happens to a few, so you can't really go by their stories, either. It's kind of like baseball. Think of all the kids who want to become big league baseball players." He paused. "Remember when you were a kid?"

I nodded.

"There are millions of kids all across America that want to be Mickey Mantle. But how many Mantles are there?" He paused and thought for a moment. "For that matter, how many baseball teams are there?" He laughed. "A lot more than opera companies. But then there are a lot more kids that want to be baseball players than opera singers," he mused. "Well, you have both the majors and the minors. Opera is a bit like that. We have the major houses, such as those in New York, San Francisco,

Chicago, and so forth, and then there are smaller companies—we call them 'regional,' sort of like the minor leagues. But even they can be tough to get into.

"It all begins with your teacher. If you can study with someone who is well connected, one who knows people, conductors, stage directors, agents, well, if that teacher likes you—and that can be a big if—he, or she, can help you. I think that's how most of us, people like me I mean, got our start—from our teachers."

"Sounds like you need a teacher that not only can teach you to sing, but can help you get a career started as well," I said.

"Oh, yes!" nodding his head for emphasis. "Well, look, kid, I have to run. I'm sure there's someone downstairs looking for a bellhop…"

Picking up the cue, I jumped to my feet, "Oh, yes, sir. Thank you, sir. Thank you. I appreciate your time," and beat a hasty retreat.

Through a fellow bellhop, Larry Flood, I met Jim DeHaven—they were high school buddies from Ocean Grove. I'd never met anyone like Jim, the finest pianist I had ever encountered up to this point in my life. He sang like a pro, too. We immediately became fast friends and he agreed to coach me. He was the first person to recognize my voice as tenor when he played for me for the first time. He made me feel relaxed, so my voice was much freer than when I sang in lessons or auditions. Singing the only thing I knew, "Comfort Ye" from Messiah, I sailed right up to the high notes with relative ease.

Jim stopped, turned to me and said, "Bob, your timbre is definitely tenor, not baritone. Those who say you are a baritone don't understand voices. I think your voice will develop into a very fine instrument. Your voice opens up as you go higher, even though you struggle with it now. You don't have enough sound on the bottom to be a baritone."

I believed him because he was an accomplished baritone, far more so than I could imagine of anyone our age. He had a polished sound like Mr. Worthington's. Unlike mine, Jim's voice had a baritone sound!

To coach me he would come to the hotel, or I to his house, and we would sing, and then talk about the future. He taught me a number of operatic tenor-baritone duets. Some nights we'd join Larry and go bar-hopping with fake IDs. Larry got one for me somehow. After a night of drinking, we three, or just Jim and I, would stumble out to the boardwalk and sing Verdi and Puciini until we were hoarse, our efforts swallowed up in the pounding surf.

We passed the summer that way: drinking; chasing girls; Jim giving impromptu concerts at the hotel; taking voice lessons with the soprano soloist at the Auditorium; dating the lovely misses staying or working at the hotel; and more drinking and singing our heads off. I was pretty good-looking and still in reasonably good shape from all the running and biking I did in high school.

For the first time in my life I was on my own and could do what I liked—within the strictures of the law, my bellhop job, my Christian upbringing, and common sense. I felt as if I were in one of Elvis' beach party movies. My afternoons off were spent on the beach flirting with waitresses from the hotel—or, for a week or so, one exquisitely lovely hotel guest who was there with her grandmother.

Beth and I met on the elevator, which was one of my jobs. It was an old elevator requiring an operator. I loved this job because it was easier than lugging heavy baggage, and I got to meet people. (Downside: no tips.)

The attraction between us was immediate. How could I not notice an attractive brunette with eyes as blue as the sky with soft bobbed hair? Her lashes flirted with me as I looked down into those eyes that drew me in like a bee to a flower. I stole a glance at the rest of her. She seemed young, but had the figure of a twenty year old cheerleader. Her dazzling smile seemed to say, "Hey, you're pretty cute!"

The same afternoon on her way to the beach, she stopped to talk (flirt) with me. I could see the concern in her grandmother's eyes. She knew she had her hands full with this granddaughter! I admit, I was smitten and flirted right back in my own bumbling way. I wonder if my naivety and uncertainty around girls heightened her attraction to me.

After she came back from the beach I was really glad to see her again. I smiled as she stepped on the elevator. Her smile was nothing less than radiant. We began talking as though we were old friends, picking up from when we last parted. When we reached her floor, she asked if I could take her down again.

"Why?" I asked looking at her quizzically.

"I just want to talk to you some more," she said, cocking her head to one side and looking up at me with those sparkling blue eyes.

Oh... Oh! Okay. I closed the door and cranked the lever to "down." When we descended to the first floor, she remained in the car. Others got on. She smiled coyly at me and moved to the back to make room. The party got off on the second floor. Hers was the fourth.

She moved closer as she asked me, "So tell me about yourself, Bob."

I told her about my singing aspirations and that I was even taking lessons this summer.

"Can I come to a lesson?"

We were almost to the fourth floor. I stopped the elevator just shy of it. She smiled as she cocked her head as she had before, taking a step toward me. "Why did you stop the elevator?" She touched my shoulder with her finger.

"Well, ah, ah, well, if you want to come to a lesson I'll have to ask…" I was going to say "my teacher," but realized that would be so very un-cool, so I blurted over myself, "I'll have to explain to you how to get there." By this time she was standing so close we were touching.

"Where are your lessons?" Again with those inquiring eyes.

I blushed and turned away as if to check on the elevator. I felt warm all over. "At the Methodist Church," I said over my shoulder. "Know where it is?" She shook her head demurely. "Then I'll have to explain."

Suddenly the elevator buzzer squawked in on our little tête-a-tête. I pushed the lever to complete the trip to her floor. As she exited I asked her to wait while I delivered the other passengers.

Frankly I did not expect her to, but she did. She not only waited, but she came to my lesson the next day. We met down stairs and walked to the church together. Much to my surprise she took my hand. No girl had ever done that before. At first I blushed, but when I looked into her smiling eyes, I was captivated holding her warm, soft hand. When we arrived at the church, Bette Benjamin, the soprano soloist at the Great Auditorium and my summer teacher, wasn't there. For a moment we stood looking into the room with the piano where my lessons took place. Beth was looking at the piano, and I was looking at her. On a sudden impulse I stepped behind her, lifting her light brown tresses off her neck, and bent down and kissed her soft neck. Without a word, in one motion she turned around facing me, threw her arms around my neck and pulled me into my first passionate kiss.

At what point Bette arrived I don't know, but we jumped apart at a very distinct, "Uh-hum!" My face must have been crimson as I introduced Beth to Bette. Bette smiled indulgently, but went right to work. After the lesson Bette departed, leaving us alone again. There was not another soul in the church even though the doors were unlocked.

Beth approached me with upraised arms and a face straight out of heaven. "Oh, Bob!" Her eyes were glistening with tears. "You have the most beautiful voice I ever heard in my life!" She wrapped her arms around my back with her head on my chest and squeezed me. I put my arms around her, squeezing her right back. She looked up into my eyes – and we were kissing again with our bodies tight against each other.

Never in my life had I received such adoration about me or my singing. I knew at that moment how much I loved this waif of a girl about whom I knew absolutely nothing.

Was this "love" about her, or about my voice?

With less than a week left to spend with her, I took advantage of every moment. She introduced me to Grandmamma and I earned her stamp of approval. The next night I took her to the only movie in town, Psycho, which had just hit the theaters for the first time in Asbury Park, the town next door. There was no entertainment in the religious village of Ocean Grove. The movie scared the heck out of both of us, but it brought us closer. We were clinging to each other by the end. After the movie we walked hand-in-hand, sometimes arm-in-arm, or arms around each other, on the boardwalk. We stopped to enjoy the surf; we took off our shoes and ran in the sand. We dashed toward the surging surf, chirping as the cool water rushed over our toes, laughing and giggling like school children. Stopping for a moment, we turned around hand in hand to look back at the boardwalk. It was eerie at night from the water's edge; the yellow lights looked like candles in a Christmas window. I don't know how long we stood there basking in the warmth each of us gave the other.

When we finally returned to the hotel, I used my key to get on the elevator, which didn't run this late. This time, as it took us up to her floor, I had an inspiration. Even through our embrace she noticed we passed her floor, threw her head back, and with a gleam in her eye queried me playfully, "Bob, what are you doing? Where are you taking me?"

I put a finger across my lips. "You'll see."

Previously I had discovered a window on the top floor that led to the roof. I decided to show Beth "my secret." She held my arm tightly. When the elevator stopped, I led her out into the dingy top floor hallway, off limits to visitors and bellhops.

To our right, one bare light hanging on the wall—as in Psycho—toward the end of the hall, trying to shine through the dirt that encrusted it, gave the place a creepy feeling. The hall grew darker the further we tiptoed our way along it.

She whispered, "Where are we going?" A twinge of apprehension showed through her smile. But her sense of adventure clearly captivated her as she interlocked her arm with mine.

I led her straight to the window case. I could hear and even feel the salty wind whistling outside. I pulled the window in and up, handing it to her to steady as I crawled through.

"Is this safe?" she whispered hoarsely above the gusts outside.

"Sure! Come on!" Standing on the ledge I helped her through. We now stood on a narrow ledge along the base of the roof at the foot of one of the hotel's majestic turrets or gables.

She looked down, about sixty feet to the boardwalk below. "Oh, my God! This isn't safe!"

There was no guard rail, it's true. But I put my arm around her, pulled her toward me, and gently turned her around so she was facing out, still holding fast to me. I held on to the window ledge with my other arm. "Look!" I whispered in her ear.

"Oh, my God!" she gasped again. But this time her words were hushed astonishment. As she looked out she saw and heard the distant dark waves smashing into the murky beach, all of which appeared dark brown from the boardwalk lights. She could see the white-flashing breakers dancing all along her line of sight.

Then her eyes were drawn back to the Homestead Restaurant, immediately across the boardwalk from us. Its roof, which she had never seen from this vantage point, appeared dark and spooky. "This way," I directed in her ear, ushering her around the front of the turret to the adjacent roof on our left, which gently sloped up to the apex of the roof in back of us.

We sat down on the roof, wrapped in each other's arms to keep warm. Shivering, we slid close to the turret to avoid the direct blast of wind. Ocean Grove was quiet, but Asbury Park was still in full bore. Its blazing, glittering lights lifted our spirits. The great Ferris wheel lights dazzled us as they whirled in their endless orbit. The clang of other rides and hurdy-gurdy music wafted shakily up to us on the ocean breeze.

We could smell the cotton candy, open-flamed burgers, deep fried French fries, and grilled hotdogs. The boardwalk was flooded with merry-makers, young and not so young, occasionally calling to one another along with the shrieks and tumbling cars of the rides. We smiled and looked deeply into each other's eyes. Her eyes were the color of a bright summer sky. Our lips couldn't get enough of the other's.

How long we huddled there has evaporated from my memory. But the next day we met to go to the beach. Hand in hand we dashed to the beach, frolicked a while in the sand and surf, but soon returned to our beach towels, she on hers and I on mine, extended end to end so that we faced each other and could hold hands across the edges of the towels.

As we held hands she asked innocently, "Bob, how old are you?"

"Twenty-one," I replied, a little too quickly. I blundered on about how complicated it was being a third year college student, but only a sophomore because of changing colleges and majors. As I talked she lowered her head. Wondering if I said something stupid, I abruptly stopped my college career blabbering and asked her, "How old are you?"

She lifted her head with the dignity of a princess and looking me straight on the eyes, replied, "I'm fifteen."

What?

My stomach knotted. Sweat beaded on my forehead as my insides froze. Everything started swirling around me. I loved her so much I thought about proposing—we loved all the same things, and she's crazy about my voice, the first person to tell me how much she loved my singing. What a support she'd be!

Robert! For God's sake, hold your horses! She's still in high school—with two or three years to go. Are you crazy? She's jail bait for you...

No! Stop it! How can you sully our love with such talk? She's not bait... She's... so young... so radiant... so charming... intelligent... beautiful... fun... and:

She taught me how to Kiss!

She loves me. I love her. What do I do now?

At that thought my central memory core crashed. I cannot remember anything about her after that beach incident other than that I wrote to her after she went home. I do not recall receiving an answer, but I agonize today about how I may have treated her after this revelation, and pray that I did not treat her unsuitably in any way. If there's any blame, it falls on me. I loved her and she loved me. Our time was out of joint.

Jim encouraged me to accompany him to New York City to audition for the Mannes College of Music. There was a famous French baritone, Martial Singher, who was head of the vocal department with whom he wanted to study. He assured me it didn't matter that I was a tenor. He could teach me, too. It felt good to know I was moving into the professional ranks. I thought about Dad and his bullying me to go his way. Would he appreciate what I had accomplished thus far?

The bus dropped off Jim and me at the Port Authority in New York. I had only three dollars in my pocket. How naïve we were! When young folks don't know that something is impossible, they just go ahead and do it. Jim was a shoe-in with his background. Unlike me they took him into the Opera Workshop this first year. Mannes accepted me as a voice major with a minor in piano. A comfort was knowing that Aunt Kay and Uncle Vin lived in Astoria. Surely they would help me if needed.

After singing for Mr. Singher, he confirmed that I was indeed a tenor. As to my future prospects, he said with a twinkle in his eye, "Well, my dear, we shall see!" He had the last say as to my acceptance at Mannes, so I felt as though I were on my way at last toward a singing career.

And you know what, Dad? Being accepted at Mannes was no "pipe dream." I did it, and I paid every penny myself, thank you very much!

At the time I was so angry with Dad that I was not connected to the length and depth of his disapproval. My anger buried the hurt deep inside. I was so used to Dad's disapproval and carping about everything I did that I didn't realize at the time just how much all of it hurt. Nor had I any connection with how that hurt drove my anger. My father was a very angry man; I blithely assumed I had inherited his temper.

Jim and I first arrived in New York in the post-Ocean Grove fall of 1960. We stayed briefly with a family we knew from the North End Hotel. When that came to an end Jim went back home to Ocean Grove while I stayed for several weeks through the beginning of school with Aunt Kay and Uncle Vin until we (Jim and I) found a small one-and-a-half room brownstone apartment on Eighty-Second Street between Lexington and Third. The living room had a bed with a slide-out cot underneath; the half-room was a kitchen with a stand-up shower nestled between kitchen and front room. These would be close quarters indeed.

The apartment rented for $96 a month, which seemed steep to us. But it was an easy walk to Mannes, which was then on East Seventy-Seventh Street. Mannes College today is located on West Eighty-Fifth Street between Amsterdam and Columbus Avenues. To make my new college life feasible, I knew I had to get a job right away—to eat and pay my half of the rent.

Chapter 4

The Long Climb Begins—Mannes College Of Music

September, 1960

All the way up on the Lexington Avenue subway from Aunt Kay's apartment in Queens, I felt a rush of excitement along with the tension of not knowing what to expect. When I walked through the front door of the Mannes College of Music that fair day in September, who could have foreseen that my life would be changed forever—in more ways than musical? But this was the real deal, as they say. It's do-or-die time, and the fear and embarrassment of possibly failing made
me think of Dad.

Damn it, I can't let him win. I've got to DO this!

I repeated it over and over to myself to buttress my confidence. This time I was on my own—no Jim DeHaven to guide and cheer me on.

I pulled open the door on East Seventy-Seventh Street to one of the finest music colleges in the country, not to mention New York City. Nervously entering the vestibule, I spied a table in the middle of the hall before me where a handwritten sign had an arrow pointing to the left:

☐ ==============
REGISTRAR'S OFFICE
============ ☐

There was also a pile of forms with another smaller sign saying:

☐ ==============
TAKE ONE AND FILL IT OUT COMPLETELY.
BE SURE TO SIGN YOUR NAME AT THE END.
============ ☐

Along the walls other students were seated filling out forms, so I found a chair and did likewise. No official-looking person appeared that I could ask what to do with my completed form. I figured other students there probably had the same question, but I didn't want to disturb them.

So, out of the corner of my eye I watched to see what they did when they finished their forms.

Soon an attractive student—could she be a singer?—completed her forms, took them to the office, came back, and sat down. When her name was called, she went in. Oh, that's simple enough. She had a big smile when she left, so I was reassured.

When my name was called I walked into the registrar's office, not much larger than a walk-in closet. There were shelves along the walls and two chairs straight in front of me placed before a wide desk or a long table—I couldn't tell, behind which sat a well-dressed, somewhat portly and matronly looking woman with a strange blond coiffure that reminded me of the rings around Saturn. As I was to learn later, this strange hair-do was her trademark.

As I entered I thought I saw her nudge the young lady on her left whose head was lowered, preoccupied with the papers in front of her. At the brief touch on her arm the younger woman looked up. Our eyes met. Hers were the most ravishing brown eyes I had ever seen. Shoulder length deep brown hair with an auburn sheen complemented a shy but winning smile. The older lady stood up as she removed her half-moon reading spectacles and let them drop, suspended on a strap around her neck, and introduced herself as Mattie, the registrar.

Her eyes had lit up at the sight of me, but glowed now that the young lady and I noticed each other. Mattie sat down still smiling. With her left hand she graciously introduced me to her assistant, Miss Joan Bishop. Mattie's eyes telegraphed Joan, "Now here's a young man for you!" As Joan blushed, Cupid danced joyously around the room.

Mattie bent over backwards to help me get settled at Mannes and in working out the details of paying my tuition, particularly since I didn't have a job yet, nor could I pay up front. I gave them what I could, and for Mattie it was enough. She trusted me to get a job and continue the payments.

When classes began, I assumed that Mr. Singher would be my voice teacher. But instead, I was sent to his voice-teaching assistant, tenor Wayne Connor, much to my chagrin. It felt like a slap in the face that said,

"You're not ready to study with Mr. Singher." That was not the first time I heard the words, "You're not ready," nor would it be the last.

Wayne reminded me very much of Mr. Pfliegger, both of whom were chiseled from the same tall, blond cast. Their voices were similar as well. Wayne had a rounder face with large blue eyes that lit up when he smiled, his features softer than Mr. Pfliegger's. Maybe it was his Irish ebullience that won me over. Sure, I felt slighted by not studying with Mr. Singher, but there was no choice in the matter, nor was it personal, so I resolved to make the best of it.

Although I have no recollection of my lessons with Wayne, he must have trained me well enough, because in my second year I moved up to Mr. Singher, my first important voice teacher.

Through the forties and fifties Mr. Singher had sung at the Metropolitan Opera and had been regarded as the French baritone of the Met roster. Peter B. Flint described Mr. Singher's distinguished background in a New York Times obituary, published on March 12, 1990. Flint said that Singher's career began in 1932 with the Paris Opera, and he came to the Metropolitan Opera in 1943. Mr. Singher himself told me that he had sung extensively in Europe and in South America—Buenos Aires in particular.

While he enjoyed his status as the leading French baritone of the Met through the forties and fifties, he sang roles in French, Italian, and German, all of which he spoke fluently. He also spoke a beautiful Castilian Spanish. Even though he suffered from angina most of his life, he died at the ripe age of 85 in 1990.

Mr. Singher carried himself like a dancer, shoulders back with his head held high. Not a tall man, he was handsome, distinguished-looking with thinning hair, and enhanced his height with his regal bearing. His clothes were stylish—everyone wore business suits in the sixties, à la Cary Grant movies of that period, although I remember Mr. Singher in tweed jackets with the leather elbows—his manner gentlemanly, and his smile warm and gracious. He was the epitome of the French gentleman. A learned man, he held a doctorate in French literature.

Lessons lasted an hour, with the first half devoted to singing technique and the latter half to repertory. Mr. Singher was the first teacher to recognize me as a tenor. He said, "My dear, I do not know why zey told you you were a baritone. Perhaps in school choirs the teachers decide based upon your range. But for us it's a question of vocal timbre, which I heard in your voice at your audition last summer. You definitely have ze tenor quality. That you cannot now sing ze high notes—well, zat's what we have to work on," he said with a twinkle in his eye. He assured me that I was in good hands because he taught a technique that came from the famous French tenor of the turn of the twentieth century, Jean de Reské, a world-renown dramatic tenor in his day and later a very successful teacher here in this country.

As soon as I could, I went to the library to look up de Reské, and felt excited to be studying with a teacher with such historic operatic connections.

"When you sing, sing into zee nose. Not 'through' zee nose, but into it. We call it 'dans le masque' ('in the mask')."

Mr. Singher demonstrated how the tone was to be directed into the mask with a sound very much like Worthington.

"Keep zee breath away from zee voice," he said, pushing his hands down his sides. "Zat way you won't tighten your chest, shoulders and throat."

Mr. Singher was at his best in the second half of my lessons because he was a natural actor and teacher. He could put you in the scene of an opera, or find the subtleties of a song that made the difference between ordinary and masterful.

I'll never forget in later years working on the garden scene aria, "Ah, leve-toi soleil" from Gounod's Roméo et Juliette. Mr. Singher verbally painted so grand a picture for me that I could see Juliet on her balcony at the far wall of the room, the rose garden between her and me, and even the wall behind me I had just climbed over to see her. With that as an introduction, I poured my heart into it. The notes sang themselves not just from my voice, but my soul as well. When I finished, Mr. Singher, beaming, crossed toward me quietly applauding. "Very good, my dear, very good indeed!" He called everyone, my dear—"Sing like that, and we shall see…"

I was so excited to be working with a world class singing teacher in one of the great music schools in New York City that I wanted to yell to the world, and especially to Dad, See? I did this myself—despite your disdain and opposition. What do you think, Mom?

September, 1961

One day early in my second year, I was sitting with the Dean of Students, Shirley van Brunt, conversing about something I've long forgotten, when all of a sudden I heard an incredible tenor voice coming from another room. He was singing "Cielo e mar," the tenor aria from Ponchielli's La Gioconda.

Shirley noticed that I was paying more attention to the voice than our conversation. Pointing in the direction of the voice, she said casually, "Oh, that's James King, having his final voice lesson with Mr. Singher before he leaves for Spoleto. James just won the Spoleto contest, you know." James King later became a star at the Met, specializing in the German repertoire. James sang 113 performances at the Met from 1966 until 1984 when he began teaching at Indiana University. He performed extensively throughout Europe as well.

No, I don't know. I later learned it was called the "American Opera Auditions," held in Cincinnati in 1961.

"And he has a contract to sing at the Berlin Opera House (next) fall. He has such a big voice Mr. Singher wanted him to sing in the hall rather than in a studio. Would you like to meet him?"

"Of course!" I almost jumped out of my skin.

"OK. Let's go."

As she got up I leaped to my feet and followed her into "the Hall" where performances took place, in the center section of the first floor. The Hall was quite modest by theatrical standards, but not so modest considering this had been the family residence of David Mannes, the school's founder.

We slipped in the door and slid along the wall to the back of the auditorium. James was having difficulty with the last high B-flat of the aria. Singher saw us out of the corner of his eye and immediately went into his "show-time" mode.

He smiled at James and patiently explained, most probably for my benefit, how high notes are to be sung: "See-ng it with a slan-der [slender] vowel. Slan-der," raising his hand, index finger to thumb, as a conductor raising his baton. "Slan-der."

"Again, please." Eventually they finished the aria.

Mr. Singher then introduced me to James, a tall, strapping fellow, with dark hair and a broad smile. He was very handsome, reminding me of the Hollywood movie star of the forties and fifties, Robert Ryan. King had a voice to match his good looks.

Mr. Singher later told me that if I worked hard enough I too might have an important career—"Not like James, of course. Your voice is not in that league. But, with dedication I can see you singing in the smaller houses of Germany, for instance. Perhaps you might consider singing as a comprimario. Many singers make a lot of money at that," he added, responding to my downcast look. This comment fell short of what I wanted to hear, but he meant to encourage me, I think.

He worked hard with me through our four years together, but always with cautiously selected words of encouragement. Certainly I learned how to sing in a large auditorium and progressed musically and artistically as well as vocally, but he continued to have reservations about my career possibilities.

From his perspective, if you are not improving it's because you're not responding to his teaching. In other words, it's your fault, not his. You just don't get it.

From my perspective, I struggled with my breath control, and the idea of keeping the breath away seemed counter-intuitive to me, yet I had added the top notes to my voice that later became the envy of other tenors.

Breath control is to a singer what bowing is to a violinist, or flexibility is to a dancer. It takes years to develop breath "control," supporting the voice so it will project into a large hall, over an orchestra—without a microphone. Diaphragm strength without tension takes years of practice until you don't have to think about it.

My breath control continued to trouble me throughout my career. At first I figured my difficulty resulted from my not being as trim as I had been as a teen, so I tried running and riding the bike as much as I could. It helped, but never seemed to be enough. There were times when I felt as if I sang like Pavarotti, but I couldn't seem to depend upon that "feeling" or "place" of singing all the time.

Other times, for reasons unknown, I struggled for breath, often needing to take breaths where Mr. Singher, coaches, and conductors forbade it.

Somehow through all this, my belief in myself never wavered. Oh, it sagged plenty of times, but my dream to "sing like Mario" never died, though by this time my sights had shifted to higher artistic goals than Mario Lanza. I strived to learn the languages I sang, to learn acting, and to sing musically. In other words, to be a "complete" singer.

By the end of 1960, Joan and I were dating steadily. Christmas was on the horizon, so we began to plan what to buy for each other. That's tricky to do when you're always in the company of the other person. Even so, Joan rushed me around to stores from Fifth Avenue to the Garden State Plaza. Since I was new to the area, Joan loved showing me her favorite haunts.

As it turned out, Joan paid for my tuition that year for a Christmas present. I was overwhelmed with gratitude. How could I ever repay a gift like that?

"Just love me," she said.

Because of our grueling schedules, Joan and I could not date, at least in the traditional sense. We spent as much time together as we could. One way was by going to the opera. The Metropolitan Opera made score desks available to students who attended music schools. These desks were lined up in two rows in the Dress Circle along the right side (from the stage) of the auditorium. They were designed for following an opera using musical scores. Researchers as well as students and other opera specialists used these lighted facilities to follow the opera.

We wanted to see the singers, observe the staging, acting, costumes, etc., rather than follow the music, so we took advantage of these desks whenever we could. We saw some of the great artists performing in the early sixties, such as Joan Sutherland, Franco Corelli, Leonard Warren, Richard Tucker, Roberta Peters, Renata Tebaldi, to name but a few. Hearing their great voices always thrilled us to the core.

One of the benefits of score desks was being able to attend operas for only four bucks. We went as often as we could. For us that was togetherness.

The tickets through the school were hard to get for the operas we wanted to see because other students also wanted them. You had to get to the bursar's office early. On the night of a performance the race was on. You'd have to run up three flights of Met steps to get a front desk that had a full view of the stage. Being in good shape, I took two steps at a time all the way up the three flights.

The first night we attended an opera together, we arrived early to edge our way as close as possible to the front of the crowd waiting at the bottom of the first floor steps. Ushers barred the grand stairway that dominated the main hall. I leaned over to Joan and whispered in her ear, "I'll go on ahead to get a good desk. Don't try to keep up."

She looked surprised, but nodded her head and mouthed, "OK."

The instant the ushers let us pass, I bounded up the stairs like a mountain goat. The people around us looked at one another in astonishment. But I wasn't the only person flying up the steps. Two other guys whom I did not recognize—probably from other music schools—also took off. But my two-steps approach caught them off guard at first, but then they joined the race for the coveted places.

More often than not I won the race, but even if I didn't arrive first, there were several desks good for viewing. Sometimes the other guys weren't singers. One time a student conductor, lugging a heavy score, took the desk beside me. Panting like a quarter-miler, he slammed his score down on the desk, and demanded of me, "What was the rush? Do you always come into the Metropolitan Opera this way?"

"Only when I have score desk tickets."

"Why? The desks are all the same."

"It's not about the desks; it's about being able to see the stage."

"Oh, Lord," he exclaimed, "you must be a singer."

Seeing the operas we loved enabled Joan and me to discuss them at length, finding the virtues and flaws in the productions. We could also analyze the singers, partly as an exercise in our knowledge and understanding of singing, but also as a means of helping cope with our doubts and fears, both singing and career-wise. This, our version of dating, drew us very close.

She had studied with Mr. Singher herself throughout her Mannes career and continued studying with him after her graduation in 1962.

As we became more involved Singher knew we dreamt of a career together. During one of Joan's lessons, at which I was present, he turned to me and said,

"Do you hear zat voice, Bob?"

I nodded appreciatively.

"She iz destan'd for a major career, I am certain. Such a lovely sound! And her diction in all languages iz pearfect. Add to zat her superb musicalité, and presto! You have an artist of ze first rank."

Turning to me, he added, "I wish I could say ze same for you, but you know," as he took in how my face dropped, "you could sing at her side."

As he said those words, he held up both his hands with his index fingers next to each other, the one higher than the other, indicating my subordination to her.

I felt crushed. The weight of my despair made my entire body feel like lead. Joan was embarrassed as well, knowing how much I yearned to sing. I wanted to crawl through the nearest crack in the wall.

Damn it all! This is like Dad all over again. But at least he threw me a bone.

One day I was working on the song, "Adelaide" by Beethoven, which I eventually sang at my graduation recital. As I began the first phrase, Mr. Singher stood up, crossed the room toward me with a big smile, and held up his hand up like a traffic cop.

"My dear," he began, "do you know what you are singing about?"

Classical singing combines great literature with great music. In the song repertoire the words (usually poetry) came first, and inspired the composer to set them to music. The words, therefore, are as important as the notes. Singher always insisted I learn the words before the music, for several reasons. One, to pronounce the words correctly in the rhythm of the music, and two, to notice how the composer set them, which tells you how to interpret the piece.

Joan has always helped me to translate French, Italian, and German texts. Part of Mannes' program for singers were classes in language diction. That week I had not had time to prepare the piece in detail, assuming Singher would help me with the parts I had not translated. But the way he asked the question struck me as an indictment. My heart pounded in a panic attack, and my mind shut down to such a degree that if he had asked me my name I could not have come up with it. Knowing I could not translate it completely, I could only say,   "Roughly."

His usual pleasant and charming face suddenly morphed into a mask of rage. Eyes blazing, his collar began to glow red as the blood soared to the top of his head. He marched over to the piano, snatched the music from the rack in front of the startled accompanist, slammed the music shut, shoved it roughly into my chest, pointed to the door and bellowed,

"Roughly? Get out of here and don't come back until you know exactly what you are singing about!"

That unforgettable lesson took me back to Mr. Fontana's "lesson," and I guess by this time I should have been used to being told to GET OUT. My father threw me out of his shop several times as well.

However, from this incident I learned something positive: to always be conscientious in preparing both text and music before presenting the piece to anyone.

Winter, 1961

In order to graduate Mannes with a degree in opera, you have to have three years of Opera Workshop. Mr. Singher and Mr. Connor would not let me join the OW my first year. "You're not ready," they declared. Not again! It took me four years to finish Mannes.

My second year, 1961-1962, Mr. Singher permitted me to join the "junior" Opera Workshop. It was directed by the Viennese-born pianist/coach/conductor Paul Berl, who had distinguished himself in the opera world as the long-time accompanist of the world renowned soprano, Victoria De Los Angeles, along with conducting and teaching in numerous important international venues. A patient teacher, I liked him and respected him so much that in my last year I asked him to accompany my graduation recital. How excited and proud I was to be accompanied by De Los Angeles' accompanist!

This workshop was designed for singers like me with limited performing experience. In the first two years of OW we sang scenes from operas like L'Elisir D'Amore, Magic Flute, and the Commedia dell'Arte scene from Pagliacci.

My first complete role in a fully staged production was Paolino in Cimarosa's comic chamber opera Il Matrimonio Segreto, ("The Secret Marriage"). We sang it in English my junior year in the spring of 1963.

The major lesson I learned from this experience came courtesy of James Lucas, our intrepid stage director, who impressed upon us, "You are not to be funny in any scene—as in Charlie Chaplin or Bob Hope funny. The comedy is in the situation, not in the characters themselves. You have to take yourself very seriously—act your parts with straight faces—only then will the opera be funny."

An important lesson I never forgot.

During my senior year, spring of 1964, James also directed my second complete opera role, Alfredo in Verdi's La Traviata. As bombastic and opinionated as he was, James and I got along well because I respected him as a fine director, and he respected my musicianship and intelligence. He never said anything about my voice or singing.

Mr. Berl coached me in this role while Mr. Singher and I worked on the vocal preparation. The role of Alfredo moved me up the operatic ladder into meatier repertoire. It was also a role I knew I would sing again and again.

I thrived in this musical, dramatic milieu, and felt as though I had found my true self. Feelings that I had buried for years surged forth onstage, especially anger (Dad) and love.

For me opera is the culmination of all the arts, and the challenge of excellence drove me to do my best. All the objections Dad had flung at me began to fade. Learning to express deep emotions through music, other languages, and coupled with the sheer physical act of singing, lifted me out of my old self and gave me a new lease on life.

Then there was the last scene of La Traviata when Violetta dies:

James insisted I pick her up after she collapses and carry her dramatically offstage as the curtain comes down. The first time we rehearsed this scene, I stooped to pick her up.

As I cradled her in my arms, I went to lift her. Something snapped in my back. I collapsed on top of her. I started to laugh, but not my soprano, a tall ample-figured girl for whom I had to wear elevator shoes in order to appear taller than she.

She opened her eyes and glared at me. "How dare you embarrass me like this?" her eyes screamed. She said out loud, "Are you such a weakling that you can't lift me?"

I froze, not knowing what to do or say. My back was pounding, my legs buckled under me.

She looked frantically around for Jim, who was standing off to the side—laughing his head off. The rest of the cast started to laugh as well—until they saw Her Face. Some became embarrassed; others looked away as they snickered among themselves.

When I realized how furious she was, my face turned crimson, and I tried to pull my arms from under her and get up. But they too felt as though I had ripped every muscle from the bone. I tried to get back on me feet, but couldn't.

"All right, all right, people!" Jim shouted as he crossed to us, shooing them aside. "What's the problem here?"

For me that was a pretty stupid question; the problem was obvious. I couldn't lift her. Period. Your question should be, what are we going to do about it?

But Jim's attention was on the soprano.

"Are you okay?" he asked solicitously.

She scowled at him, and then slowly nodded her red face. She was about to speak when he turned to me and shouted,

"Are you going to do this or not? What's your problem?" as if I had refused to follow his direction.

By this time I was on my feet, and ignoring Jim, I reached down and tried to help her up. "I can do this...but not tonight!" I sheepishly muttered to him as I continued to assist her.

"OK, everybody! We've had enough for tonight. Go home!" he bellowed. "Get some rest." He never asked me whether I could actually lift her; he wanted it, so it had to be done.

So I began a weight lifting regimen in earnest. But subsequent rehearsals made it clear I simply couldn't do it. I implored Jim,

"We have to restage this."

"What?" he exploded. "I want you to lift her. If you can't do it I'll get someone else."

If there was another tenor—or even just another stronger guy who could lift her, he didn't care. But Mr. Berl insisted there was no one to replace me, so James had to relent for the production to go on.

I suggested that I gather her in my arms and cradle her on the stage floor as the curtain came down. To my surprise, he liked it.

"Good, Bob. That works very well." The show was a success after all.

Mr. Berl was the music director and pianist for both operas. James Lucas went on to an international career directing operas, plays, and musicals in major houses both here and abroad. Mr. Berl, as I indicated, was already a well-established artist.

In the Meantime...

Already in the summer of 1961 Joan and I were very much in love and determined to get married. Our parents were not very keen on the idea with me still in college.

"Why don't you wait until you finish college and get a job?" was the familiar refrain.

In order for that to happen, I had to demonstrate to both families that I could earn a living and support a family. Of course I wanted to do that through singing, but clearly I was "not ready."

So back to the working world! My career as a library page lasted less than a year because an opportunity arose to become a clerk at the music branch of the NYPL, then located on Fifty-Sixth Street just off Lexington Avenue, within walking distance of both the school and our apartment, albeit a very long walk, but entirely feasible for this young guy who loved to run.

In fact, the year in which I took a class in music history, running the eighteen blocks from Mannes College on East Seventy-Fourth Street to Fifty-Sixth Street became a necessity. Mrs. Catherine Miller, chief librarian of the music branch and my boss, put me in charge of the NYPL Orchestral Collection, a unique collection of orchestral music available to qualifying amateur orchestras. Open only on Wednesdays from 12:30 to 4:00 p.m., I nevertheless worked 17½ hours a week, 3½ of which had to be these hours. My class in music history ended at 12:30. The eighteen blocks suddenly loomed much longer. I couldn't run that fast!

"Do you think we could push the opening time back just a smidgen?" I asked Mrs. Miller.

"No," came the solid but polite reply.

When I asked Dr. Braunstein, my music history professor, "May I leave class a little early on Wednesdays?"

He clearly forgot his European manners, "Vat? Leef early? Nefer!"

Mrs. Miller, a softy at heart, agreed to look the other way if I opened the collection no later than 12:45.

No problem, but it put my running to the test for two semesters. I was in excellent shape in those early days. At the time I weighed 135 pounds.

Some of my borrowers were memorable characters. Studying people became an intentional pursuit of mine because observing others helped me to create characters for the stage. One such character was Irving Byer, an elderly, wealthy insurance salesman who owned his own agency.

He was short and bald and had considerable difficulty with the two flights of stairs in that old Carnegie Library building. The collection was on the second floor while the "circulating" branch of the Music Library occupied the first floor. There were no elevators, so the couriers had to carry the heavy bundles of orchestral music up and down two long flights of marble steps.

The familiar scrape of his shoes shuffling laboriously from one step to the next announced his arrival. Before he came into view, Byer would stop about three steps from the top and wearily call out, "Doctor Mitchul, so vot haf you donn fear me lately?"

The first time he greeted me I was furious. Doctor indeed! And who was he to demand favors of me? I was the guardian of the collection, and he, as I was soon to discover, consistently left the musicians' pencil marks on the music—against library rules. He should remove them, not I.

But Mr. Byer could disarm me with his lively sense of humor and self-effacing manner. As I got to know him better, he would always ask about my family, loved to dispense advice about proper diet and, when he learned I was a singer, had the sure cure for a sore throat. Some of his mannerisms ended up in my Kaspar in Amahl and the Night Visitors: the way he slogged up those daunting steps, and the way he cupped his ear when he missed something I said.

Another orchestral borrower was the Mannes College. One day Maestro Carl Bamberger himself showed up. Bamberger was the resident conductor of the Mannes Orchestra and the Chair of Instrumental Music, and, unknown to me at the time, a conductor at the New York City Opera. Bamberger was the big cheese on campus who ruled his domain with an iron fist, including the orchestra and the Mannes Opera Company.

He intimidated me. And had I known he conducted at City Opera, I would have behaved very differently.

The Mannes Orchestra, an amateur orchestra, borrowed music from the collection. The regular courier, a young blond fellow, carried the bundles on a bike. How he did it mystified me. However, he ignored the no-marking-the-music rule, and I always gave him a hard time about it.

Then came that day when Bamberger himself trudged up the steps with the music. At first I thought it was Mr. Byer. What a surprise! I recognized him immediately, but how did he know me? Seeing me, he was astonished.

"Oh! It's yuu," he said. He seemed to know me by sight but not by name. "I expekted to see a fery old mann mit two beerts from all zey tolt me about zee seveere Mr. Mitchull!"

He dumped the packages on the table, pulling imaginary beards on either side of his face. He laughed at his own joke.

Bamberger himself. What's he doing here? He's too important to do this job...

As if answering my unspoken question he began lecturing me about how essential it was for his orchestra to mark the music, and how he resented that he could only keep the music "for two veeks," grousing that the next time they borrowed the music all his marks had been erased.

When he ran out of steam I patiently explained that Mannes is not the only orchestra using the music. Other conductors had their own markings, so the NYPL decided that each orchestra remove all markings before returning the music.

Outraged, Bamberger tried to convince me that his markings were the only correct ones, so his should be allowed, indeed, preserved by the library.

"Zat vay eferyone vill be happy," he insisted.

I was about to shout at him, "Who the hell do you think you are?" But I bit my tongue and told him that he must think all other conductors are nincompoops, a presumption we cannot support. Besides, these are the NYPL rules and all users must abide by them. "In fact," I continued, "I have in my file a copy of the agreement you—or someone from Mannes—signed, agreeing to the rules."

He would have none of it, but thinking he signed it himself, I began rummaging through my files to retrieve it—to stick in his face. As I did so, I muttered over my shoulder that he must abide by the rules like everyone else. Bamberger, a well-known and respected conductor with a colossal ego, not to mention being born in Germany where youngsters do not speak that way to their elders, stormed out in a huff.

I was left standing there, heart pounding, sweat pouring down inside my shirt. I wanted to scream after him, but my mind raced through numerous scenarios of my being called on the carpet both at Mannes and at the library. I sat down to wipe my brow with the nearest muslin wrapper.

As the weeks passed, none of my doomsday scenarios materialized, and by and by I forgot all about it.

However, a year or so later I had another encounter with the redoubtable Bamberger, this time as a singer. Somehow I had been selected to sing the role of a one-person "chorus" in a Lucas Foss opera called Introductions and Goodbyes. On the one hand, being under Mr.

Bamberger's direction meant that I had moved up to the senior opera workshop; on the other hand, after reviewing the music, I wanted to scream.

This one-act chamber opera became my worst nightmare. My recollections of it vary from its description on today's web site. However, I love the following web quote: "The opera's prelude begins with a disjunct [sic] and pointillistic [sic] melody that spans a range of six octaves." The two words, disjunct and pointillistic sum up precisely my opinion of the music: it was (and still is) unsingable, certainly by me. Why did he choose me for this?

Playing the role of a one-man Greek chorus that comments on what's happening onstage, I sat in the pit right under his menacing baton. Disjunctive and pointillist translate to popping out staccato notes from top to bottom of one's range, a wrecking ball for the voice.

This music has no harmonic structure, "atonal," meaning, "without reference to harmony." To make matters worse, the orchestra plays something totally unrelated to what I sing, making it impossible for me to find my pitches. Only a person with perfect pitch—a gift enabling a person to hear and sing any pitch from memory—could sing this, a gift I do not possess. Few people do.

To this day I cannot fathom why Mr. Bamberger selected me to sing this—except perhaps that his sister, Gertie Bamberger, who was Mannes' solfeggio instructor, told him I was a star sight-reader. In any case, I felt as though I was in the middle of the ocean—without a boat.

All through rehearsals Bamberger stopped to correct my wrong notes. How could he hear that they were wrong? Almost any note, high, low or in between, would have fit, or matter very little even if you could find them. He must have had perfect pitch himself—?

Just the thought of attending a rehearsal made me break into a cold sweat. By the time the performance rolled around I was a nervous wreck. You can't imagine my relief when it was done. I scooted out before the reception rejoicing, Thank God that's over!

This experience was certainly the lowest point of my budding opera career. Undoubtedly it put me on the bad side of the maestro because he never again used me for anything, operatic or otherwise. I have often wondered if he recalled that Orchestral Collection incident, and if this Foss assignment was some sort of retribution.

Back to Joan and me

"Goodbyes" affected my appetite. When Joan and I first met I was already pretty skinny. I topped the scales at 135 pounds, probably less after "Goodbyes." She always thought me starving, so early on she appointed herself my Florence Nightingale by bringing me lunch every day. We became inseparable and did everything together—except live together. It simply was not done in those days, at least not in families like ours. We went to movies, concerts, and the opera, and dreamed of becoming the darling couple of the opera world, singing together in operas like La Boheme, L'Elisir d'Amore, Faust, Manon, and others that featured soprano and tenor lovers.

It wasn't long after Joan launched her lunch campaign that her mother wanted to meet this mysterious man in her life. So, I was invited for a Sunday dinner at the Bishop home in Fort Lee, New Jersey.

I traveled by bus to the Palisades Amusement Park—now occupied by high-rise apartments—where Joan greeted me with a radiant smile as we walked home. Like a little kid, I couldn't wait to see her and be with her again, especially in her home and to see where she grew up.

Mom's admonitions about being polite and respectful when in other folks' homes made me nervous, but all went well. Fred and Johanna Bishop made me feel very much at home, and the dinner was fabulous. The conversation concentrated mostly on my background and family. Occasionally I asked questions about their family, which were answered generously. At the end of the evening Mr. Bishop drove me back into the city, with Joan along for the ride.

Many subsequent visits were made easier by Mr. Bishop, who often picked us up at Mannes after school and elsewhere in the city after a concert or an evening at the opera. In the mornings, Joan took the bus into the city to her secretarial job, and then the subway to Mannes or another meeting place after work. Her parents did not like her taking public transportation home in the winter season when it got dark early. That was the reason for Mr. Bishop's taxi service.

After several months I became a weekend fixture in the Bishop household. Joan's parents fixed up a spare room in the attic for me so I could stay over on the weekends when possible. It felt cozy for me to have a family once again to come home to.

All this while there was never any talk about marriage. I think the Bishops would have freaked out if there had been…

It wasn't long before our relationship began to get serious. I was not Joan's parents' first choice. They would have preferred somebody with better prospects, someone who had a good job and a solid career path; an aspiring musician had neither. Even teaching would be better, but performing still carried the stigma of "unstable" to most adults of that generation.

But Johanna loved me nonetheless, and fed me very well—too well in fact. At first Fred and I had some difficulty in relating. As with most fathers and their daughters, he was no doubt suspicious of my intentions, although he never would have said so. But we became fond of each other, and soon I was calling them Mom and Dad. Still no talk of marriage, though.

My weight went up by fifty pounds over the next couple of years. Mom Bishop dispensed love on a plate. Eating when I was growing up was a privilege, and seconds were discouraged. "Save some for another day," was the Mitchell maxim. The Bishop motto by contrast was, "Bob, have some more!" I thought I had died and gone to heaven. Those pounds snuck up on me.

By Christmas of 1960 I had given Joan a turquoise ring as a token of my intention to marry her. It was also to show Dad Bishop that my intentions were serious.

The following summer of 1961 I worked very hard back in Lock Haven for Johnny Yost, a funeral director and family friend for many years. When I was in high school he gave me a job on his landscaping crew. I also helped him in the funeral business. He even began to groom me to take over his business some day.

I had earned enough money for tuition that summer, but I had other plans: I took five hundred dollars of it and bought Joan an engagement ring to surprise her. Never mind how I would pay my tuition—I was madly in love. The only thing that mattered was to surprise her.

Time had run out for me to return to New York by car, so I flew to Newark Airport where Joan met me. It was a blistering, sunny day. While waiting for me she had moved to the passenger seat, preferring that I drive. As soon as I got into the car, I said, "Close your eyes!"

"Close my eyes?" she asked suspiciously. At first she looked puzzled, but immediately a smile brightened her face, like a child anticipating a birthday present. She dutifully folded her hands in her lap and closed her eyes. I reached into my pocket and brought forth the dream-filled packet. I had planned this moment, but when it came, the pretty speech zipped right out of my head. I held the small box toward her, opening it to reveal the precious, emerald cut diamond that I now held it in front of her face.

"Okay, you can open your eyes now."

It was so hot in the car that her face glistened with sweat, while my hands were so slippery the tiny box almost slipped out of my shaking hand. She opened her eyes. "Oh-h-h…!" was all she could utter. Her mouth dropped like a stage trapdoor. Her eyes could have lit up Broadway. She turned to me, her face now so wet with tears and sweat I couldn't tell which. Who cares? She fell into my arms and we enjoyed the wettest kiss we ever had.

"Oh, Bob! It's beautiful! Thank you, darling. Oh, God, I'm so happy! Thank you! Thank you!"

By this time I was crying, too. She handed the ring box back to me and asked me to put the ring on her finger. As I fumbled with the box I nearly dropped it, but managed to get the ring on the correct finger of the correct hand—she made sure of that.

I don't remember actually popping the question, nor that she actually said, "Yes," but it was a done deal nonetheless.

Even with the purchase of the engagement ring, my college tuition dilemma worked out. Mattie, our intrepid Mannes registrar, devised a payment plan for me. She, after all, was our Cupid, and it was not in her kind nature to do anything less. The following year, on September 9, 1962, Joan and I were married at the Leonia (NJ) Presbyterian Church. Mom and Dad, my brother Johnny, Uncle Vin and Aunt Kay all came to the wedding. Originally, I wanted Johnny for my best man, but he told us they would not attend the wedding because they were serving alcohol. So I had asked Cousin Paul to be Best Man. The family had a great reunion, but we missed our two sisters who could not afford plane tickets. Johnny's arrival was a pleasant shock.

"I'm embarrassed," I confided to him. "I'd already asked Paul, months ago…"

He held up a hand, cutting me off. "Think nothing of it, Robert. I understand. Couldn't be helped. Just think. I don't have to think up some stupid toast for you." We laughed.

"How'd you get the money to come?"

"Some very nice people in my [French] congregation took up a collection."

"Wow!" We hugged enthusiastically.

Joan, who had graduated Mannes in June of 1962, said she got her BS in June, her MRS in September, and two years later, when I graduated, her

PHT ("Put Hubby Through"). She worked as a secretary, and I continued my job as a clerk for the New York Public Library in charge of the Orchestral Collection. We set up housekeeping in West New York, New Jersey, at 5907 Boulevard East, on the corner of Sixtieth Street. Our apartment building overlooked the Hudson River and the New York City skyline, just opposite Sixth-sixth Street in Manhattan.

Our future lay just across the river.

Fall, 1963

In the fall of 1963, I took a philosophy course with Dr. Eckstein. This day he was late for class. He was never late. We waited patiently, murmuring among ourselves, expecting him to fly through the door at any moment. He was a self-professed rabbinical dropout who had made an indelible impression on me. In a private moment after a class he told me he came that close, pressing index finger to thumb, to becoming a rabbi, but decided he just couldn't buy into the God-thing. His integrity forced him to change course and complete his doctorate in philosophy rather than in rabbinical studies. "Cost me a lot!" he quipped, remarking how much more money he could have made as a rabbi.

Suddenly he appeared at the door. His customary cigar was in his hand instead of his mouth, and he shuffled into the room rather than bounding in with his usual energy. His suit looked as though he had slept in it, not totally unusual, although it looked frumpier than usual. His dark hair seemed ruffled, but that too would not have caused us to stare at him with disbelief. From beneath his heavy, dark-rimmed glasses I thought I saw a tear trickling down his cheek. Now that caught our attention; Dr. Eckstein was as upbeat a man as you'll ever meet.

He stopped midway across the room and announced,

"The President's been shot. Go home."

And he turned on his heel and walked slowly back through the door. I thought I heard him sobbing as he disappeared down the hall.

President? Who? Mr. Mannes? [President of Mannes College] Shot? Looking from one face to another, we asked each other, "What did he say?"

"Did you hear that?"

"No, what did he say?" The subdued murmuring continued for a minute or so until we slowly came to the realization that it was President John F. Kennedy that Dr. Eckstein was talking about.

"Is he dead?"

"How should I know—Dr. Eckstein didn't say."

"Wadda we do now?"

"He said to go home…"

I sat bewildered, not knowing what to think. First one student got up, followed by others; eventually we all filed into the hallway to see others filing out of their classrooms. The hush was uncanny. Typically the corridors would be filled with a cacophony of conversation. But not today, November 23, 1963. It felt like a strange dream to me, not knowing, yet knowing something catastrophic had happened.

We all went downstairs and gathered in the front room, whispering disbelief to one another and looking for information. Someone asked if anyone had a radio. Another suggested a trip to a local bar that had a TV. Soon a group went out in search of a TV.

My first thought was to call Joan, being newlyweds. But she was at work and I didn't have that number with me. I walked out the front door of Mannes just to get away from the rising throng. Some people claimed it was a hoax and we should go back to class. Others said no. But people on the street that normally ignored each other now looked sadly at anyone who caught their eye and said, "Did you hear? The President's been shot." Another would question, is it really true? Someone else answered, "Oh yes, it was on TV. Go look! They're showing it over and over."

But is he dead? No one knew. They had rushed him to the hospital and thought he would survive. Many whispered, "Thank God!"

I took a subway to the Forty-Second Street bus terminal. Even on the subway people buzzed, "The President's been shot!" As I waited for my bus upstairs in the port authority, no one knew whether or not he was dead. Suddenly I noticed Joan also on the queue for our bus. I joined her so we could ride together. On the way home, a young passenger with a transistor radio got the news that President Kennedy had died. From there the ride home to West New York was even more somber. We both cried.

After arriving home, even the day off seemed unreal. We watched TV for as long as we could stand it, and then took a walk along Boulevard East. Hand in hand we came back to the park across the street from our apartment and sat on a bench watching the New York skyline, barely talking to one another. We both felt the pain everyone in the country felt that day. Losing a president felt like losing a very dear loved one—whether you liked him or not. It wasn't about JFK. It was about the presidency itself, and how some nut could do such a thing. What's the matter with us? We had all failed as a nation. The euphoria of the fifties was over.

Spring, 1964

When it came time for my senior recital in 1964, after two operas Mr. Berl and I had worked together quite a bit, and now we were spending many hours working on my ambitious recital program. Inspiration for some of the program came from Johnny's recording of Jussi Björling's September 24, 1954, Carnegie Hall recital. Both Mr. Singher and Mr. Berl offered suggestions as well.

THE MANNES COLLEGE OF MUSIC

157 East 74th Street, New York, 21

Monday, April 27, 1964   8:30 P.M.

Graduation Recital by ROBERT MITCHELL, Tenor

Paul Berl, Piano

Program I

Purcell	.	.	Man is for the Woman Made
Gluck	.	.	O del mio dolce ardor
Durante .	.	.	Danza, danza, fanciulla gentile

II

| Schubert . | . | . | Frühlingsglaube Ganymed |
| R. Strauss | . | .Freundliche Vision Heimliche Aufforderung |

INTERMISSION

III

| Koechlin. | . | .Si tu le veux Fauré Tristesse Aurore Prison |
| Chabrier . | . | . | Ballade des gros dindons |

IV

Vaughan Williams .   Four Hymns
Lord! Come Away
Who is this fair one?
Come Love, come Lord
Evening Hymn

Thomas Molloy, Viola

In the fall of 1963, my last academic year at Mannes, Mr. Singher had become head of the voice department at Philadelphia's Curtis Institute of Music. I didn't want to start with a new voice teacher who would make me start all over again. But traveling to Philadelphia every week was a pain—and expensive. We also didn't know whether Mannes would approve.

We decided to ask and were granted permission to do so. The trip was initially grueling but soon became routine.

My recital that fall didn't garner rave reviews by the New York Times—no reviews at all, actually. But the applause was hearty enough to please me. I even received a couple of bravos for my rendering of Tosti's, "L'alba separa dalla luce l'ombra" as an encore. After a long program it was a daring piece to attempt. Joan thought I was terrific. I too was proud of what I had accomplished, especially when you look at the path that led up to this point. I was optimistic about the future.

But dangling over my head was the ever-present problem with my breath control. How could I overcome it? Maybe a new teacher could help. Joan and I discussed the question of a new voice teacher—how do you shop for a good voice teacher? Whose advice can you trust?

My graduation was in June 1964 with Congressman John Lindsey as speaker. At the time he served Manhattan's Seventeenth District, but he covered the speaking circuit to enhance his bid to run for mayor, a post he was to occupy for several terms starting in 1966. The only thing I can remember about his speech were his slurred words betraying the kind of lunch he'd just had. I don't remember what he said, but I remember how he made me feel: embarrassed.

All I had accomplished so far meant nothing to my parents; they didn't come for any of my performances, even my graduation recital, or the graduation itself. "Can't afford it," my father blustered, noting both the expense of the trip and time off from work. By this time my hurt, buried far underneath my anger, remained dormant—

Recently a friend mentioned how hurt I must have been by my father's obstinate disapproval. I had remembered only my anger, not the hurt that caused it. After all these years the realization of my pain hit me hard.

Aunt Kay, now a widow, came to my graduation recital, the only family on my side to do so. The Bishop family was there, of course. But my brother Johnny was just beginning his fifty-plus-year missionary work in France, coming home every six years; 1964 was not in his cycle. Our sister, Joan, lived in Hawaii, and Cis lived in Indiana at the time, too far away for these occasions.

Graduation was my last hurrah at Mannes. I felt greatly blessed to have enjoyed the opportunity to work with the best artists opera has to offer. My teachers were prima and taught me how to make music on a professional level. Because we sang mostly European operas, having European teachers and coaches helped us learn the languages and styles correctly. They were pros themselves—"been there, done that"—so we knew we were getting the best musical and vocal instruction available.

Hey, Dad! Am I still your tinker's damn?

Lock Haven, Mansfield, and now Mannes, all lay behind me; my future stood before me.

Where do we go from here?

Chapter 5

Where Do We Go From Here? Spear Carrying A City Opera

New York City Opera
Fall, 1964

One summer prior to my coming to New York, Joan had studied with Mr. Singher at the Marlboro Music Festival in Marlboro, Vermont. There she met luminaries like pianists Rudolf Serkin and his up-and-coming son, Peter Serkin, City Opera mezzo-soprano Marlena Kleinman, and Met soprano Benita Valente.

As it happened, when she was in New York, Benita took occasional lessons with Mr. Singher at Mannes. By the time I arrived on the scene, Mr. Singher had invited Joan and me to one such lesson. From these contacts we were able, after my graduation, to ask both Benita and Marlena to advise us about our careers. Help us get started, maybe? Both of them graciously listened to me sing, having already heard Joan at Marlboro, and told me that I "wasn't ready" to sing opera.

Not again! What's this mean? It's so frustrating. I've sung two leading roles on stage. Doesn't that count for something? What about the getting into the Metropolitan Opera Studio?

Sidestepping my questions, they urged us to find a good teacher who could prepare and help us find our way into the opera field. Marlena herself later became one of the premier singing teachers in New York, but in 1964 she was singing at City Opera and not yet teaching. She recommended that we contact Mme Olga Ryss, "a great teacher," she said. In addition, Marlena helped me get a job as a spear carrier (supernumerary actor or "extra") for the fall 1964 season at City Opera.

It wasn't until 1966 that City Opera relocated to Lincoln Center. In 1964 they still occupied their own theater on West Fifty-Fifth Street.

"Don't ever sing in the chorus," she counseled, "because you'll never get out. Once a choral singer, always a choral singer." She also advised me against singing small parts. Carrying a spear was okay because no one notices supers, she said.

I was ecstatic. Being associated with City Opera I knew I would meet the "right people" to get me into the opera field. I was sure Marlena would help, and maybe Benita could get me in the Met. My naïve optimism was never higher.

So, from October 1 to November 15 that year I carried a spear at the City Opera of New York, ever hoping to be discovered—by somebody—somehow…

This is how I remember that experience:

Maybe I could ask baritone Sherrill Milnes, who's making his debut tonight—October 18—in the role of Valentin in Faust to help me. Dare I ask him?

Right now I'm standing backstage next to Sherrill just before our first entrance. He's very nervous, I can see that. Nope. Definitely not a good time. I doubt he would remember us even though Joan and I saw him just a week ago in a concert he gave at Tenafly High School in New Jersey. I was very impressed with his singing and gorgeous voice. It was a thrill to go back stage and meet this up-and-coming baritone. I thought about asking him then, but I neither knew how to broach the subject, nor whether it was proper.

As we await our entrance I turn around and smile up at him, nearly a head taller than I. He smiles. I say, "I don't know whether you remember me from your concert last week in Tenafly."

He nods.

I beam that he remembers me. Pointing my finger at him authoritatively, I say, "You're going to be the next Leonard Warren." Warren was the leading baritone in the world during the forties and fifties.

He blushes shyly, shrugs his broad shoulders, and says, "Ah, shucks! Thanks a lot." He's genuinely touched. I pat him on the arm and turn around as I hear our entrance music.

What a thrill to march on to the stage of the New York City Opera. No worries about remembering my lines—I don't have any. I just have to march to my rehearsed spot. He marches behind me, but passes me on the way to his spot down center stage. The lights are blinding, the orchestra loud. When the audience sees Sherrill they begin to applaud: his arrival at City Opera has been much heralded. From the corner of my eye I can see the mixture of exhilaration and nervousness in his face as he goes by. Soon after he enters he sings his big aria, "Avant de quitter ces lieux." I'm standing only a few feet behind him to his right. When he finishes, it sounds as if the whole audience jumps to their feet. They roar,

"Bravo!" and "Bravissimo!" They clap their hands, they stamp their feet. The ovation continues, seems at least five minutes. I can feel his goose bumps in mine. What a glorious moment in operatic history.

And I am here.

In 1965 Milnes debuted the same role just across the Lincoln Center Square at the Met, launching his glorious international career. My prediction about him was right: critics indeed compared him to the great Leonard Warren.

Also in the cast were bass Norman Treigle as Méphistophélès, and Marlena Kleinman as Siebel.

Norman Treigle had a splendid bass voice, powerful and rich, yet with a hard edge Joan and I attributed to his smoking. A consummate actor, he reminded me a bit of actor Jeremy Brett, with his cutting voice, chiseled features and lithe body. Norman could move on stage like no other. I wondered if I could ever do that as well as he did. His flexibility was amazing, and he could sing while dancing a jig. He also appeared in Don Giovanni, Carmen, and Boris Godunov that season, as did I.

In fact, there still is a costume somewhere in a City Opera warehouse with my name on it—unless it was lost in that terrible fire a few years later. I was one of four bodyguards for Boris in the English-version production especially mounted for Norman, and I had a costume made just for me. I remember the fittings—I felt like a pro. Hey Dad! Look at me! They're making a costume just for me—custom-fit!

Boris got a lot of press, deservedly so, and I was proud to have been part of it.

Being a bodyguard to Boris, I got to hang around with Norman backstage. One night as we were chatting prior to an entrance, Norman told me he had studied with Robert Weede, the great Met baritone of the forties and fifties, perhaps more widely known for creating the role of Tony in Most Happy Fella on Broadway.

"Weede taught me all I know," he said. I can't begin to describe how important I felt rubbing elbows, sometimes literally, with such stars as Milnes and Treigle. That night in my backyard pleading with God to sing like Mario seemed comically naïve. There I was, on the City Opera stage, fraternizing with major opera stars. I felt as if I had made it.

But then my voice of doom, dear Dad, my Jack, chimed in, Hey Stupid! You're carrying a spear, not singing. I could almost hear a satanic chuckle.

Thanks for that icy reality check, you SOB. Did you have to spoil my feel-good moment?

Opening night of Boris has its share of hitches, but Norman gets a standing ovation as the critics write frantically. After the performance the entire troupe, it seems, tromps across Fifty-Sixth Street to the Carnegie Tavern. Joan meets me there, having attended the performance. We order roast beef sandwiches with Russian dressing—in honor of the Russian opera. The beef is thick, the bread heavenly, the beer delicious, and the Russian dressing unexpectedly perfect with roast beef. That sandwich becomes our instant favorite. Several friends sit with us, all gabbing at once: Florette Blank, Mme Ryss' assistant and our second teacher, along with other students of Flo's.

Just about the time the beer and sandwiches arrive, Norman makes a grand entrance into the tavern, a noisy entourage at his heels. He sweeps in like the tsar he has just portrayed. With all eyes riveted on him, waiters stop and turn to him, patrons jump to their feet like a flock of birds soaring skyward in a tightly packed swarm, all of us applauding and cheering his fabulous opening night. His second standing ovation lasts longer than the first. Our hands are sore from clapping; our voices hoarse from cheering. What a moment!

In the Don Giovanni production, Norman alternated in the title role with baritone John Reardon, probably better known for his appearances on Mr. Rogers' Neighborhood. It was strange seeing this man close-up after seeing him so much on TV. Little Rob loved that show.

Donald Gramm, a former student of Mr. Singher, sang Leporello. According to Mr. Singher, he had worked with Donald at the Music Academy of the West in Santa Barbara. Yet I felt a kinship to him, knowing the Singher connection. I watched his every move and luxuriated in his glorious bass sonority, wishing I were a bass instead of a tenor. He was so good onstage! I laughed my head off from the wings at the way he did the Catalog Aria. In this aria Leporello recounts the Don's bedroom conquests for Donna Elvira, one of his many jilted mistresses.

Beverly Sills sang the role of Donna Anna most impressively. Hers was a strong, bright coloratura voice which could spin out pianissimo high notes. Her high B-flat on "abbastanza per te" in the recitative before "Non me dir" took my breath away. In 1964 she was a young roster singer at City Opera, stunningly beautiful, reminding me of a young Lucille Ball.

It would be a few years until Sills sang the Donzetti queens that catapulted her to international fame and glory.

A story to remember, at least for singers, was the performance of a young tenor in the part of Don Ottavio. Apparently, Julius Rudel, conductor and general manager of City Opera at that time, had permitted this young comprimario to try out a leading role. As I was standing in the wings waiting for the next act to begin, Mr. Rudel came behind the closed curtain discussing this young man's performance with the stage director. Rudel's bass voice, which could pierce armor, enabled me to hear his remark all too clearly: "Once a comprimario, always a comprimario." Ouch! That stinging rebuke has remained with me all these years, a cliché that affirmed Marlena's advice not to sing small character roles.

The last opera I was in was Carmen, in which a number of singers alternated in the various roles. Norman Treigle usually stole the show as Escamillo. But on October 25 a really beautiful, petite, young soprano, Joan Gavoorian, debuted as Micaëla. She shone with her sumptuous voice, graceful acting, and sheer feminine beauty. For such a petite woman she had a surprisingly rich Puccini voice, and with her stunning beauty, I figured her a sure bet to go straight to the top.

But a few months later, on February 8, 1965, she and another singer, mezzo-soprano Lillian Garabejian, happened to be on Eastern Airlines Flight 663, which crashed during takeoff from Kennedy Airport, killing all eighty-four on board, a great shock to the opera world. I was greatly saddened by this terrible loss. Joan and I knew Ms. Gavoorian personally, as she sometimes substituted for Marjorie McClung, the regular soprano soloist at Central Presbyterian Church where we sang in the all-professional choir. Ms. Gavoorian was a sweet, approachable young lady, unlike many sopranos-on-the-rise I have encountered.

Sherrill Milnes wrote in his book, American Aria: Encore, that he too was scheduled to be on that flight, but "some personal business came up at the last minute" causing him to switch to a later flight. Thank God.

Speaking of tragedy, Norman Treigle died a few years after I met him of an accidental overdose of sleeping pills. Norman had been the basso of City Opera for twenty-three years, and there was talk about his going to the Met. He was already known internationally and had recorded on important labels. I was fond of him personally because he treated me as an equal, rare in opera circles. His generosity of spirit made me feel as though I were a part of his opera world, like a colleague, even though I knew he knew I was not.

Being a hick from the sticks, as I thought of myself, every night I had to pinch myself to be sure this was real. It was a dream to be onstage in a company like this. True, I never sang a note at City Opera, but I drank in all that was going on around me. Some people, especially Norman, had a way of raising me to a different level, one that I had longed for, but feared I could never attain. I think he would smile at what he had done for me.

+++

In the Carmen production, I was onstage only in the first and last acts. So I had to wait upstairs for over an hour to go on again. There was a special room in the upper reaches of the old opera house for the supers, one for the men, another for the women, unlike Amato's. Most of the guys spent the offstage time gossiping.

Growing weary of it one night, I ducked out to explore the upper regions of the house, much as I had done in the North End Hotel. In a hallway off the beaten track, I chanced upon an unlocked door and opened it. It was dark and I couldn't see a thing. As my eyes adjusted, just inside the door I looked down and could make out a catwalk that snaked along the wall. Looking straight out I became aware that it was high above the stage where the performance was going on. Cautiously, I put one foot on the narrow footway. I reached out for something to hold on to, and my wrist caught a metal cable that swayed when I touched it. My hand quickly grabbed on to it.

Why in the world is this door unlocked? This is dangerous!

As I carefully stepped on to the narrow catwalk, I could see it was twenty or thirty feet above the stage floor. I still couldn't see very well, but sensed there was nothing between me and the stage below. My grip on the cable tightened. Through the hanging scrims and curtains I could now see the stage and hear the ongoing performance wafting up in an eerie way, partially muffled by all the hanging curtains and scrims.

Soon I became absorbed in a magical musical moment during the entr'acte between Acts II and III. It begins with the harp, followed by a solo flute spinning out a haunting melody. A clarinet echoes it, followed by the strings as it soars to its climax. From there it descends into a quiet end, the same solo flute sounding the last, diminishing note. What an exquisite little piece. I had never heard it played so well, before or since, carrying me into an unforgettable, enchanted world, all my own. Music does that for me.

Applause broke the spell. It was so enthusiastic I edged toward the front of the stage along the catwalk to see who was conducting. Expecting Maestro Rudel, I was surprised to see Charles Wendelken-Wilson in the podium. My goodness! Joan and I knew him from Mannes and the Central Presbyterian Church on Park Avenue, where Charlie was the assistant organist. I knew he was working as some sort of an assistant coach or conductor at City Opera, but had no idea he conducted major performances like this. I was thrilled for him.

Unbeknownst to me at the time, Mr. Rudel taught conducting at Mannes, and Charlie was one of his students. Remembering what Frank Worthington told me in Ocean Grove about the importance of teachers helping to start careers, my mind started racing…could Charlie help me?

As I continued to watch the next scene, I thought back to a night when Charlie stopped at Jim DeHaven's and my apartment on East Eighty-First Street. He came primarily to see Jim, a close friend. I was in the kitchen cleaning up and Charlie quipped from the other room, "Why Bob, you're just so domestic!" His remark, which has stuck in my head all these years, infuriated me because I was angry with Jim for not helping me keep the apartment livable, so angry in fact, that I stomped out in response to Charlie's remark.

As I stood there on the catwalk admiring his performance, I imagined what a great conducting career Charlie would be destined to enjoy—he was that good.

My rash behavior that night flashed through my head. Forget about it, I thought.

The idea was never tested: our paths never crossed again. In 1975 Charlie began a lifelong career in Dayton, Ohio, where he distinguished himself as conductor of the Dayton Philharmonic Orchestra and the Miami Valley Symphony Orchestra. He guested at City Opera and Wolf Trap.

Suddenly I awoke to the fact that I had to rush back to the supers' room to line up for the last act.

+++

Entr'acte

June, 1966

Six, Six, Sixty-Six, a day that was out of joint for the Mitchell family.

Dad! Stop this "nobody-cares" nonsense. Of course, Dr. _____ cares. Get your butt over there and quit that stupid heavy lifting job. You KNOW your heart can't take it …

What? They won't let you off to see the doctor? Do you want me to come up there? I'll kick a few butts. Tell them to go to hell and get yourself to the doctor. Now!

Aunt Mary? Why are you calling? What happened? Where's Mom? Why can't she come to the phone? …

"It's about your father…"

… Oh, no! …

Dad died from the last of a long series of heart attacks he had over the years. We drove to Lock Haven to say goodbye and to be with family. I was still with the New York State Employment Service. My brief stint at T. J. Lipton and my thirty-year career at Scholastic were still to come. So far Dad was right. I was doing what I had to do: working a nine-to-five job.

Dad, the hurt and anger we both carry can now never be undone. You took yours to your grave, but I'm consigned to lug mine around like Marley's chains. I'll spend my life trying to prove you wrong. Is this a good motivation to make a career in singing?

At age twenty-seven, my clock is ticking relentlessly.

Chapter 6
Metropolitan Opera Council Auditions

1971

I tried in various ways for a good many years to get into both City Opera and the Metropolitan Opera. Early in my career in 1971, I applied for and was granted an audition for the Metropolitan Opera Regional Auditions. At that time there were sixteen regions across the country. Singer friends and teachers advised me to sing in one of the more remote, far-flung regions so I wouldn't have to compete with the heavy-hitters— well connected, well supported contestants—in the major metro areas like New York, Chicago, and San Francisco. But New Jersey as well as Pennsylvania was part of the Eastern Region, the hub of which is New York City, opera's world-wide center. Even by claiming my parent's address in Lock Haven, we were still in that region. Cissy lived in Indianapolis, the Chicago region, and Joan lived in Hawaii at the time, the San Francisco region. One would have to reside in those regions to claim them. In addition, the Met Council most likely had ways of discovering address trickery. My family had not the resources for such a deception— even if we wanted to.

A letter arrived in the mail:

You have been scheduled for a preliminary hearing for the Eastern Regional Auditions...

Date: January 11, 1972

Time: 3:45 PM

Place: List Hall [Metropolitan Opera House in New York]

I think I sang "Qual Destino," ("Ah, mes amis" in the original French) from Daughter of the Regiment (Donizetti), but whatever it was, it must have been good because a letter dated the following day said:

We are delighted to inform you that our judges have selected you to enter the Eastern Regional Final Auditions which will be held on February 22 in the Julliard Opera Theater at the Julliard School of Music.

"You will receive a letter giving you specific details within the next three weeks. Meantime, if you have any questions, please call this office.

It was signed by Louise Williams, Executive Secretary, Regional Auditions, the same person who signed the first letter.

You can imagine my elation. The chance of a lifetime! It was like winning the lottery. I danced around the room. I called friends—everyone I knew, in fact. Already I imagined myself singing on the stage of the Metropolitan Opera with world-famous singers. It was one of the happiest moments of my life.

Hold on kid, it's only an audition, whispered a voice. That's just Jack talking, I told myself.

Over the next days and weeks I prepared musically, physically, psychologically—every way I could. I sang. I ran. I chose my best arias and worked on them with teacher and coach, conferring with them how best to perform them on the Julliard stage—which I had never seen, but how different from other stages could it be? I lifted weights to strengthen my breathing mechanism.

Even traveling to my job at Scholastic every day (since 1968) now seemed like waltzing on air.

Until…

A second letter arrived from Ms. Williams dated February 3, 1972.

It read:

Confirming our telephone conversation, our judges would like you to return for a rehearing by the Regional Auditions Committee in List Hall on Wednesday, February 16, at 4 p.m. You may sing any arias you wish, or repeat those you have already sung. An accompanist will be provided, or you may bring your own if you prefer.

There was something wrong. Why did they tell me I was accepted into the regional finals? Why the three week delay in telling me I had to audition again?

I have wondered to this day if there was some internal political struggle going on they wanted to keep under wraps. Perhaps some powerful person, a conductor, a singer, a well- known, influential teacher, or financial supporter of the Met had a singer that missed the initial audition and someone had to be sacrificed to place them in the finals. It sounded like a set-up to me. The lack of an apology and their tight-lipped attitude toward me also suggested a cover-up.

The day after I sang again, I received a letter:

We regret to inform you that the judges did not select you to return for the Eastern Region [sic] Final Auditions.

Thank you for giving us an opportunity to hear you and we wish you every success for the future. Sincerely, Mrs. C. F. Gimber, Regional Director, Eastern Region.

How quick off the mark they rejected me this time. Another reason I suspected foul play. Interestingly, they enlisted the Council Regional Director to sign this letter. I wonder to this day why they sent me the January 12 letter in the first place.

I was furious. I ranted and raved. I called Louise Williams again and gave her an earful: How could you put me through such an emotional roller coaster? I don't believe a "mistake" was made. One doesn't make mistakes like this at this level. What the hell is going on? Why won't someone at least apologize, and offer me some sort of consolation prize, like free tickets, or better still, coaching with a Met coach? At least have the judges tell me why they didn't select me so I can correct the deficiency. In past competitions judges have always been ready to do so.

Louise deflected me as best she could without commenting or answering any of my questions.

So, I sent Mrs. Gimber a letter dated February 17, 1972:

Dear Mrs. Gimber,

As you know, I have been eliminated from the competition. This is especially distressing to me in view of the January 12th letter from Miss Williams informing me that I had been selected for the Eastern Regional Final Auditions. Much to my astonishment, I received a telephone call on or near February 1 to the effect that the letter had been a "mistake" and I must sing again on February 16th, at which time I was immediately eliminated. I hope you can understand that I find it very difficult to see how such a mistake could have occurred, and that it took three weeks for someone to correct it. I would appreciate your personally looking into the matter and explaining to me what happened.

Also, I would appreciate having the judges' comments so that I know what area I must work on for the future.

Thank you for your consideration and your graciousness and encouraging words to me on January 11. Sincerely, Robert P. Mitchell

She never replied, nor did anyone contact me. Can you blame me for smelling a rat? I decided to sue them. I consulted a lawyer friend who said, "Bob, even if you have a case, what is it going to get you? Do you imagine the Met would hire you after you sue them?"

That advice broke my spirit. Shattered though I was, I continued to apply over the next several years. In 1974 I had my coach at the time, regionally known conductor Larry Newland, sign my application. In 1975 my application was signed by Mme Ryss. That was my last try to get another Council audition. Thereafter I wrote to Met administrators and even to James Levine himself. All to no avail.

Then came 1978.

Friends of ours, Edgar and Janette Green, with whom we had sung for many years at the Hebrew Tabernacle Synagogue, had retired and moved to an adult community in New Jersey. Over the years Edgar had formed a choral society that he conducted. That spring he planned a concert for which he invited me to sing as their featured soloist. The concert would be followed by a supper. Joan was also invited.

During the course of the usual post-concert greetings a lovely elderly lady, who clearly knew her own mind, approached and asked me very matter-of-factly, "Why aren't you singing at the Met?"

At first I bumbled about how hard it is to get recognition in this field, but stopped myself in mid-sentence and blurted, "Why don't you write the Met and tell them about me?"

She beamed and firmly replied that she would. And she did. Beula Silverman was her name.

August was brutally hot. That's how I remember the day on which I was to audition. Since my contact with the Met had petered out several years before, I knew the invitation must have been a result of Beula's letter. This would be my last hurrah, a do-or-die opportunity.

Joan thought the Met must have believed the letter came from Beverly Sills, whose real name is Bel Silverman. Her theory is possible, but I doubt it, otherwise my reception would have been very different.

Often in my career, when I had an important audition or performance, I would get sick. Nerves, of course: I called it my "psychosomatic custom." Normally I don't catch colds during the summer. But for this occasion I had come down with the flu. I should have rescheduled the audition, but was terrified I would never get another one after all the hoops the Met had put me through previously. This was my one and only remaining opportunity, no doubt of it. When the day came, I got up out of my sick bed and trudged into the city.

Arriving at the Met backstage door underneath Lincoln Center, I feel dreadfully weak, my legs barely supporting me. After attempting to warm up my voice at home, I decide to save what was left of it for the audition. "Zilch" reads the internal confidence meter.

Several people bustling out the stage door almost knock my head off as I try to enter. Once past the front door I see people rushing to and fro, others standing and talking, others seated on the blue cushioned chairs and sofas, yakking away.

We singers are oral people; when we're not singing we either talk or eat! Are they all auditioning? How long will I have to wait?

A guard accosts me and wants to know what business I have here.

"I'm here for an audition."

He motions me toward a glass enclosure resembling a movie theater ticket booth. Behind it is an attendant with long dark hair and dark clothes. My turn comes; the attendant, without ever looking up, studies a list of names. I tell him (or her?) my name. He finds it, crosses it off, and mutters, "Have a seat," still with his head down. I cross back toward the door, occasionally looking back, curious about the gender of the person. Can't tell.

Of course, there is not a seat to be had. I lean against a wall space taking in the buzzing scene before me. On the far side of the room two attractive women chat in front of an elevator. The taller one looks very familiar, her hair just done, dressed to the nines, her bright blue eyes and radiant smile brightening the scene. The second woman also is a model of sartorial splendor with every hair in place. They must be auditioning, I think to myself. The taller of the two, who looks vaguely familiar, seems to lead the conversation, talking loud enough that I can hear they are rattling on about their husbands, dogs, and lovers.

Suddenly the elevator doors open. The attendant says, "Miss _____ ?" I didn't catch the name, but they did. Smiles of recognition, and they stride inside. The doors close. I grab an open seat before someone else does. Only a few seconds until the elevator doors open again. A voice calls, "Mr. Mitchell?" I jump up and hasten to get on. I conclude I'm right about them auditioning.

Down, down we go into the bowels of the Met. One does not expect the Metropolitan Opera House to have so many floors, especially down to the center of the earth. We must go down about four or five levels. The elevator doors open: a chill hits me. Not good, flu and all—I sing better when I sweat, everything relaxes. When I'm cold, everything tightens.

The attendant points me down a barren hallway enclosed in yellow, prison-like cement blocks. After a few interminable twists and turns I come to an intersection. Diagonally across stand two large doors that look like an entrance to a high school gymnasium. A sign above identifies the Lower Orchestra Rehearsal Room.

In front of the open doors my two ladies talk animatedly with a young man who probably listens to the auditions. Next to me is the only chair in the hall, so I sit down. They don't notice me.

Lots of kissy-kissy, lovey-lovey, how-are-you-dahr-ling, then, "Oh, Mignon, it's always so good to see you. You were superb the other night in Aida... etc. etc."

Of course! No wonder the tall one looked familiar! She's Mignon Dunn, the mezzo star of the Met, the rage these days. I know her from pictures and seeing her on stage as Amneris. Now I get it. Mignon Dunn has just accompanied the other gal to an audition.

How am I going to follow this? Why can't there be a level playing field for singers? Where's my celeb in shining array to accompany me to auditions and influence the judges?

They enter the hall. Miss Dunn even went in to "preside" at the audition itself, undoubtedly touting her friend as she sings.

What I hear of the gal's singing through the doors sounds very good. They ask her for a second aria. Then a third. Each one is an eternity for me. After a long silence the doors open to another flurry of chatty, kissy-kissy, lovey-lovey, we'll-be-in-touch, etc. This time there were three young men who came to the door to bid farewell.

Another eternity before the women leave. The young men go back in and slam the doors shut while I sit there in the cold air. I begin to shiver. After a time the doors suddenly burst open.

"Mr. Mitchell?" shouts one of the young men—as if there were a mass of people gathered outside the door. He looks around as if these phantom folks were lined up clamoring to get in.

I'm right here, look around and you'll see me!

I stand up. Now he sees me. He turns on his heel and disappears into the room, leaving one door slightly ajar. I step through the half-open door, trying to look dignified and confident. The shiver returns as still more frigid air hits me. Everything tightens.

The room, about the size of a gymnasium with two basketball courts, has orchestra chairs, large mats, and music stands scattered around, but just in front of me is nearly empty space. To my right about twenty feet, the three auditors sit behind a long table, still talking about how wonderful Mignon looked, what she was wearing, her hairstyle, etc.

Straight ahead of me, also about twenty feet away, the bored accompanist leans across the keyboard of a large concert Steinway looking absently down at the keys. No one speaks to me. I walk over to the piano as commandingly as I can and open my score of Werther to the aria, "Pourquoi me Reveiller?" and place it on the music rack, startling the pianist.

"Shall I begin?" he asks me in a conspiratorial whisper.

"Not yet," I reply softly. With my eyes I indicate the garrulous trio that has yet to acknowledge my presence. We wait as I begin to break out in a cold sweat.

Suddenly they stop talking and look at me with fierce eyes that say, "So what are you standing there for? Sing already!" They still have not spoken a word to me.

I mention casually that we were just waiting for them.

They give me a face that says, "Just who the bloody hell do you think YOU are?"

One of them inquires absently, "What are you singing?" He really could care less.

I tell him. He waves "Go ahead already!" with the back of his hand.

I begin to sing. Immediately I know I'm in trouble. My voice is cold, my chest tight. I can neither feel nor hear my voice properly in this unfamiliar space with soundproofing on the ceiling. I get hoarse after two measures and feel as if I'm singing under water. The nightmare gets worse. By the end of the aria I'm struggling, my high notes have abandoned me, and I know I've lost my listeners, as they're back to talking among themselves.

After the final note they keep talking as if I weren't there. I had hoped to sing a second aria, which means they want to hear more. The gal before me sang three arias. Well, since I was feeling so down, and my voice had already shut down, I would have declined graciously, citing my poor condition with the flu and all... After several agonizing moments, suddenly one of them looks up, and discovering that I am still standing in front of the piano as if I were going to sing another aria, he glared at me, "Are you still here? Tha-a-a-nk Yo-o-u!"

The old Kiss-of-Death Thank You, the one that says, "Good-bye, good luck and get out of my sight." The terrible trio immediately resumes talking as though I had rudely interrupted their favorite gossip gabfest.

I turn to the accompanist, thanking him as I pick up my music. He smiles meekly as if to apologize for their horridly rude behavior, but says nothing. I face the door, mustering as much dignity as I can, considering I was in fact scurrying away with my tail between my legs. The only good thing to come out of the experience is to be back outside in that heat. Never has ninety-plus-dripping-wet degrees felt so good.

I'd let Beula Silverman down, shuddering at the thought. I'd so wanted to write her with the good news. More than that, I let myself down. Maybe Dad was right all along. As I shuffled back through the Lincoln Center complex to Sixty-Fourth Street where I had parked the car, I stared at the sidewalk, thinking, I blew it—and I'll never get another chance. Even with the heat, I felt a chill run through my exhausted body. My flu symptoms, headache, tight chest and runny nose, came back with a vengeance. After getting into the car I sat there, in the sweltering heat, not even sweating, wondering, Where the hell do I go from here?

The long trip back to Bergenfield felt like a Holocaust death march. I felt totally worthless. I needed something to take the pain way, so I stopped at a bar on the way.

"What's the problem, Buddy? You look like you've just lost your best friend."

"Worse."

"Worse? Waddya mean?"

When I told him about the audition, he muttered, "The Met, huh? Wow, you must be pretty good to sing there."

"Yeah, but not good enough."

"Oh, don't worry. You'll get another chance. They all give y-…"

I gulped down my drink, slammed the money on the bar, and walked out. I had wanted to shout at him, You're just like everybody else. You don't get it. You just don't get it. You people have no clue what it takes to sing opera. What's worse is you really don't care. You can't imagine in your wildest dreams what it took me to get this far in my singing career – in my life. And now it's over. You don't get second chances…

Back in the car I threw my arms over the steering wheel and bawled my fool head off. I don't remember how I got home.

"How'd it go?" Joan asked as I came in the door.

"Don't ask," brushing past her and going straight back to the bedroom.

"Was it that bad? Is there anything I can get for you? Some tea? You look terrible. You shouldn't have gone."

That touched a raw nerve. I wanted to lash out at her, too, but I knew she was right, so without a word I quickly undressed and crawled into bed. I didn't know what to say to her. Now I felt stupid for going, but I also knew I would never get another chance—I had to go, so what's the use of arguing about it? I blew it, that's all. I'm a failure. What can I say?

I was so angry at the Met and the whole damned system of who-you-know that I wanted to vomit all over them. That was it for the Met...

Chapter 7

A Trip to Germany

Fall, 1971

As persistently as I tried to develop my breath power, it always came up short for singing. While still a student at Mannes, Joan and I saw the great tenor, Franco Corelli, at the Met in Act 1 of Puccini's Turandot, sing her name, "Tur-an-DO-O-O-O-" on a high-A. After hitting the note, while still holding it, he struck the upstage gong three times with a large mallet, set it down, then walked downstage the twenty or so feet to the prompter's box, put his foot up on it, and held the note a bit longer. It was thrilling and unbelievable if you'd told me about it. But I heard it—witnessed it—myself.

After the thrill wore off, that feat—or stunt—really discouraged me. I couldn't hold a note for a tenth that long. How could I come close to that?

First of all, I could follow Marlena's advice and find a good teacher, one who could do something about my tight-chest breath. Marlena had recommended Madama Olga Ryss, the teacher of Jennie Tourel, a fabled international mezzo-soprano whom Mme Ryss had met years ago in South Africa. After they both came to New York sometime in the fifties, Mme Ryss took Tourel under her wing and helped her vocally to revitalize her waning career. Surely Mme Ryss could help us.

She took us under her tutelage in her small apartment which doubled as her studio on West Seventy-Eighth Street just behind the American Museum of Natural History. Her rates were surprisingly reasonable, so we decided to work with her, rather than other teachers we were considering.

After hearing me sing, she declared, "You're not ready! It takes years to build a voice..." and told us all about how long it took her students to be ready to sing in German opera houses, and of course, we had to hear about her baritone who was singing at the Met.

So I hunkered down for the long haul. What could I do? I was reduced to vocal scales and exercises at age thirty-two. When I asked her about possible roles I should prepare, she flew into a rage.

"Roles you vant? Go buy bread!"

Her sarcasm had a certain unpleasant charm, but I decided to suck it up. Even after several years with her, when I told her Tony Amato offered me Alfredo in La Traviata and that I had already sung the role at Mannes, she shouted, "Tuu dra-MAH-tik for you!" a refrain that dogged me throughout my career. "You push your voice too much. You vill ruin it singing roles like dat. You must learn to float zee sound."

All right—back to the dock when most singers my age were halfway around the world.

Mme Ryss was an enigma. In one breath she insisted, "You're not ready!" In another she said she realized how much Joan and I wanted to sing together. She knew Germany was the place to start. So, she pointed us to an agent by the name of William Stein, well known to aspiring singers, but not on a par with firms such as Colbert Artists Management or Columbia Artists Managements. Stein specialized in taking young singers to Germany.

Joan and I auditioned for him on February 25, 1971 with the understanding he would be our guide for an audition tour of Germany. We had no children at this point, so we excitedly planned our singing careers in Germany—together, or separately in houses close to one another. We felt we could hone our crafts there.

During World War II, most of the German opera houses had been damaged or devastated by the terrible Allied bombings. Many German singers were lost as well. In the fifties and sixties, as Germany began to rebuild, American singers were welcomed and financed by the Marshall Plan through Fulbright scholarships and the Amerikahaüser program to sing in German theaters and opera houses, which were being rebuilt one by one.

Unknown to us, by 1971 that welcome had worn a bit thin. Foreign singers were still hired, but the situation was completely different. I can illustrate the change by sharing my conversation with our first German agent, Friedrich Paasch in Düsseldorf, who asked me straightaway, "Have you sung at City Opera, Herr Mitchell?"

Without hesitation I responded, "Herr, Paasch, if I had sung at City Opera I wouldn't be here!" From our perspective, Germany was preparation for City Opera.

Herr Paasch was both astonished and annoyed at the remark. For him, City Opera was preparation for singing in Germany. And he, like all Germans, detested American cheek.

When we had met with and sang for Mr. Stein on that February day, we understood that he would accompany us on an audition tour of German opera houses to be selected by him. Very shortly after our first meeting, we received a letter dated February 26 stating:

"May I suggest that you look at the various scores first and decide then and there, without consulting anyone else, whether the parts are right. Do phone me when you have made a decision, so that we can take the next step from there."

This letter bore no relation to our conversation from the previous day. I was already in a tizzy because he asked me to prepare Mime in Siegfried and Froh in Das Rheingold, Wagnerian roles that I never envisioned singing, anytime in my life. My first thought was, "Sing Wagner? Me? With Wagner how dramatic can you get?" Naturally, I wanted to discuss this turn of events with Mme Ryss, but his letter said not to. If Mme Ryss thought Tamino was too dramatic for me, how would she react to my singing Wagner? The thought of her reaction numbed me. Since it was she who had recommended Mr. Stein, I wanted her to be aware of the difficult position in which he placed us. His letter concluded:

"This is rather contrary to what we talked about yesterday, but I have a reason why I have amended and re-edited my thoughts. Cordially, William L. Stein."

We never learned that "reason." Joan and I felt apprehensive about Stein's way of doing business. I did not respond as he requested, nor did we discuss the matter with Mme Ryss until weeks later. In April we received a letter with his financial terms, which we had not discussed previously. We were not prepared for the expense, even though he claimed he was giving us a sizable discount.

Shortly after receiving that last letter, Stein left for Germany with other singers he had lined up. Upon his return in June he asked us to sing for him again. In response he withdrew his support for Joan in a June 25 letter. He decided to represent me, but "there might be a slightly different approach necessary."

We were beginning to feel manipulated, so we mapped out a way to disentangle ourselves from Stein without nasty repercussions. Fortunately we had not signed any agreements, so we told him that, after consulting with Mme Ryss, we were postponing our trip. He agreed that was a good decision.

We then began to plan the trip on our own. That was difficult and risky because we simply didn't know what we were doing. Over the summer of 1971 we researched and contacted as many houses as we could, a laborious task in those days before the Internet, using catalogs, magazines, and the library. We lined up auditions with German agents as well as opera houses. It took several months of dedicated work, writing, telegraphing, and occasionally telephoning contacts, but finally the trip materialized.

We left for Germany in early October 1971, landing first in Reykjavik, Iceland, via Icelandic Airways, the most economical way to fly to Europe at that time. The terminal, a Quonset hut actually, was under construction with equipment strewn all over the place, causing me to fear for my voice in the frigid wintry air and for our safe passage. But the next day we flew to Luxembourg without incident where we rented a car and drove to our first stop in Düsseldorf to see Herr Paasch.

We also looked up our friend, mezzo-soprano Gwynne Cornell, who was singing at the Düsseldorf Opera at the time, hoping she could help us in some way. We had sung with her for nearly ten years when we three were soloists at St. Paul's Episcopal Church in Paterson, New Jersey. But we were able only to talk with her briefly in the street because of a mix-up of schedules between her and Joan's family with whom we were to meet in nearby Krefeld, who had offered to put us up for a few days.

***

Gwynne debuted at the Met in 1978, but died suddenly and unexpectedly on October 31, 1984, of a cerebral hemorrhage, just when her international career was starting to blossom.

***

From Düsseldorf we traveled to see several agents in Frankfurt, Munich, and Vienna.

Herr Starke in Frankfurt liked Joan's singing and referred her to the opera house in Pforzheim. The director of the Pforzheim Opera thought Joan's voice, while a good instrument, was in between the light and heavy roles for which he had openings, so he decided not to take her. In the meantime, Dr. Raab in Vienna thought I had strong possibilities and wanted me to sing in both Linz, Austria, and in Oldenburg, Germany.

Once again my dreams of a professional career soared.

By now we had run out of time and money. I did not want to risk losing my job with Scholastic, so we flew back home to protect it. During the following week I negotiated with Scholastic to fly back for the two auditions that Dr. Raab had arranged for me. Scholastic agreed to let me go if I took the time off without pay.

So off again I went on my second Icelandic Airways flight to Luxembourg. From there I traveled by train to Linz. From the long flight, the time zone discomfort, the anxiety concerning the shaky deal with Scholastic, missing Joan dreadfully—plus, she speaks German far better than I do—and because I couldn't sleep on the plane, I was exhausted. And I felt as though I were coming down with a cold. That was all I needed for the upcoming auditions. I could feel the old tightness creeping into my chest. How much was nerves and how much infection, who could tell?

Oh, great!

For Linz I sang Rodolfo's aria from La Boheme in German, but I was not happy with my performance, nor did they seem to be. Disheartened, I decided to take an overnight train to Oldenburg, thinking that the rhythm of the wheels clacking along would lull me to a good night's sleep. It would also spare me both a hotel bill and a day's delay in getting there.

What a mistake! The clacking rails through the night became a jackhammer in my head, nailing me in the back on the hard and narrow shelf they called a bed. Every time the train rounded a bend, I reached for a non-existent handle—as if riding in a car—to keep from rolling out of bed. My mind fermented doubts about this trip, driving me to toss and turn all night.

When I arrived in Oldenburg the next morning, I took a street trolley to the opera house. On the way there I encountered a group of high school students, some busily chatting while others tried to study. I noticed their textbooks were in English. Peering over one student's shoulder I saw the text was about J. F. Kennedy, so I decided to try out my German.

"Kannst du dass auf English lessen?" ("Can you read this in English?") I inquired, pointing to the text. "Verstehst du dass?" ("Do you understand it?")

"Ja, sicher!" ("Yeah, sure!") he replied.

So I asked him to read for me. I was surprised how hard it was for him to read the English words. Then he asked me where I was from.

"Ich bin Amerikaner," I said.

"Wirklich? Ich hätte geglaubt, dass Sie Engländer wären!" ("Really? I thought you were British!") His response delighted me because it meant I had a British accent rather than an American. This was very important for singing in Germany. Americans were scorned at the time because of a current flap about getting rid of all the American military bases in Germany, of which there were many—and had been there since World War II.

Speaking German was a priority for me because during our first trip, we visited our friends from Mme Ryss' studio, tenor Michael Trimble and soprano Vivian Thomas, husband and wife team that sang with the Karlsruhe Opera (Karlsruhe Oper) at the time. We did not see Vivian, though—she was in the hospital having their second baby. Michael said to me, "If you want to sing in Germany, you have to speak German well, both onstage and off, and especially backstage. They will not speak English to you even if they can! And God help you if you don't understand what's being said to you. You won't last a minute here!"

His warning ratcheted up my anxiety about singing in Germany.

When I finally arrived at the Oldenburg State Theater (Oldenburgisches Staatstheater), I discovered that I was not the only applicant for the one tenor opening they had. In fact, there were six other tenors there: another American resident who spoke German fluently, a Swede, a Hungarian, a guy from Portugal, and two Germans. The opening was not for a particular role or series of roles, but to be a rostered singer of the opera house—that is, a salaried employee who did not have to worry about where his next job was coming from. Even today, that's a major advantage of the German system for fledging singers.

In preparation for any audition I had lined up, I received a serendipitous lesson in German when Joan and I were in Vienna on the first trip. We happened to stay at a Gast Haus owned by a very gracious and charming elderly couple. Turns out, the wife had been an opera singer, quite well known in Austria many years before. She overheard me fretting about singing Hoffmann in German. I had sung the aria in English and French, but in Germany and Austria you sing everything in German. Well, our hostess graciously volunteered to help me learn and memorize the German text of the "Kleinzack" aria from Hoffmann. She spent many hours with me, drilling the German words, and providing interesting background stories. Her help prepared me to sing "Kleinzack" in Oldenburg, for which I am eternally grateful.

When it was my turn to sing, I first sang Rodolfo—in German, and much to my delight, they asked for a second aria. Despite my fatigue, my high C was quite spectacular, if I do say so myself. For reasons I cannot explain, my chest was open and my voice felt like Pavarotti's. The request for a second aria was a good sign, so I offered the "Kleinzack," which also went very well, thanks to my angel in Vienna. I knew I really nailed this audition since I was the only contestant to sing a second aria.

Afterwards, several of us went out for a beer. Communication among us was a riot. The Swede spoke good English, but no German. The German who came with us spoke no English. The Eastern bloc singer spoke a little German and a little English. I don't remember how the Portuguese tenor communicated with us—sign language, perhaps?

We had a surprisingly good time, and after a few beers conversation became much easier. Suddenly my German vocabulary improved, and no one cared about grammatical and pronunciation mistakes. We clinked our glasses and our voices rose to the occasion.

Just then the American tenor (the one fluent in German) came to announce that the role we all traveled from the edge of nowhere to win went to the other German singer. When he mentioned his name, I groaned.

On our first trip, Joan and I attended a performance of Die Fledermaus at the Vienna Folk Opera (Volksoper Wien). The Alfred of that evening was the very person who stole the role out from under us. We all agreed that he sang the worst of any of us, and it wasn't just the beer talking. I concluded they hired him because of his performing experience in Vienna. No doubt the fact that he was German helped as well.

My two trips to Germany were quite an experience. I got back home in time to sleep for two days before going back to Scholastic. I was really bummed out for failing to get that job in Oldenburg, especially because I knew I deserved it by singing well. The town was small and picturesque; the opera house itself was a charming old building with a relatively small stage and auditorium, an ideal venue for me. I loved the ambiance of that historic town. It would have been great to live there. Plus, being on salary meant that I could bring Joan along and we could even start a family, something we both wanted.

Drat. Well, maybe next time. Trouble is, there won't be a next time for Germany. Scholastic would not let me go a second time, of that I'm sure. My boss made it clear that I would have to choose between a marketing career at Scholastic and singing. Tough choice, not one I even wanted to contemplate. I wanted to sing, but, in lieu of a financial backer, I needed the job. And I didn't see one of those anywhere in the picture...

Back to the drawing board.

I have this recurring dream: I am to make my debut with a major company, but I can't tell which one. Old house. Lots of frills edging the balcony. Cantor Ehrenberg is the conductor. Place is packed. Agents, directors, conductors, impresarios, press … the works. I walk out on stage to sing my big aria. Can't remember what opera it is. L'Elisir? Rigoletto? I never finished learning the ensembles in Rigoletto, please, God, don't let it be Rigoletto. The music starts. I never heard this music before IN MY LIFE. WHAT IT IS? Oh, my gawd…!

I wake up in a pool of sweat…heart pounding…

Chapter 8
Aspen, and Then

Summer 1972

I returned from Germany tired and discouraged. Mme Ryss saw it immediately. "I told you so. You're not ready. Vat you need is study. Bob, let me ask you, can you and Joan come to Aspen this summer?" She was referring to the Aspen Music Festival, where she'd taught every summer since the fifties.

I did not want to derail my career at Scholastic, so I did not tell them the true reason why I wanted the month of July of 1972 as vacation time. What I told them must have been good, because July was always a busy time for our department, but they let me go anyway. Joan simply left her job at George Armstrong & Company and would look for a new one in August.

Arriving in Aspen, we checked into the house Mme Ryss rented every summer. We were part of a cadre of students she'd brought with her from New York. She taught us every day, we ate together, we played together, walked, rode bikes—and enjoyed a rest.

Joan and I took several excursions in our abundant free time. One was to see the fabled Maroon Lake underneath the more famous triple peaks known as the Maroon Bells. Another trip was up a series of three very long ski lifts ending on top of a mountain at 12,000 feet. Altogether the ski lift rides totaled five miles. I took a picture of a sail plane eyeball to eyeball, thinking all the while that the pilot needed oxygen at this altitude. Up to this time in twelve years of marriage Joan and I had not enjoyed so much time together. It did wonders for us.

Vocally speaking, the summer was devoted to hard technical work. Mme Ryss was especially concerned about my "nasal" singing she called "Nah-ZAL." I never did understand what she meant, and she would fly into a rage when I questioned her about it. She thought I was being cheeky, and I could not convince her that I was only trying to correct the problem. I finally gave up questioning her—it wasn't worth the fuss.

Since we were not students of the Aspen Festival we did not perform. All in all, July in Aspen was a very pleasant respite from our big city, year-round routine.

When Mme Ryss returned in September we resumed our lessons, but this time she insisted that I take a lesson every day. She saw the panic on my face. "Don't vorry! I vill not break you." In fact, she refused to take a cent from me. We were overwhelmed by her generosity.

Later in the year, I asked her, "Now tell me. What do I owe you?"

"Respect!"

Chapter 9

Performing at Last!

Fall, 1973

In the fall of 1973, I had two opportunities to sing important roles. The first was Hoffmann in Offenbach's Tales of Hoffmann. This role is far and away more difficult than Alfredo, and any role I had envisioned for myself. Agonizing whether or not to undertake it, I asked myself, Should I defy Mme Ryss over it? Surely she would scream from the rooftops, "Tuu dra-MAH-tik for you!" She wanted to protect my voice from singing too heavy a role.

"Dramatic" is an operatic voice category. Think boxing: Dramatic = heavyweight; lyric = lightweight.

At age thirty-four I was painfully aware that major singers, by the time they were thirty, already had ten years' experience in regional and major houses. Do I wait for Mme Ryss' permission to perform, or do I step out on my own? I did not want to antagonize her, nor did I want to seem ungrateful for the year of free lessons she had just given me.

Mme Ryss, please, my clock is ticking—away.

The story of how I solved my Hoffmann conundrum begins with St. Paul's Episcopal Church in Paterson, New Jersey, where Joan and I were soloists at this time. We had become close friends with Thomas Williams, organist and choir director. If you were to meet Tom you'd have thought he was a high school kid, typically dressed in worn jeans and a white shirt that seemed a bit large for him. Light brown hair and eyes, slight of build and height, what he lacked in physical presence he made up for with a bubbly personality. When he sat down at the organ or piano, his playing erased any doubts about his artistic maturity and seriousness.

About this time he had moved to a comfortable apartment in upper Manhattan to live by himself, just down the hill from Hebrew Tabernacle Synagogue where Joan and I sang. We were part of a professional quartet—which the German-speaking congregants called, Das Chor (choir).

Tom had become my accompanist during those years, and it was convenient to go to his new apartment to rehearse, which boasted a nine-foot grand piano occupying most of his otherwise sparse living room. Prior to living in this apartment, Tom lived in a mid-town apartment that he shared with several other musicians, including pianist and conductor, Raymond Fowler, whom I did not know.

One Sunday morning at St. Paul's, Tom mentioned to me that Ray was preparing a production of Offenbach's The Tales of Hoffmann with the Middlesex Opera Company, and he was looking to cast several tenor roles.

Although I had never heard of the Middlesex Opera, I immediately got in touch with Ray and explained that, as much as I would like to, I would not be able to try out for the title role because my voice teacher would forbid it, but perhaps he would consider me for one of the many smaller parts in Hoffmann. The role of Frantz particularly interested me because he has a short aria, and it is also a comic role, always appealing to me. Since I had studied Hoffmann's "Kleinzack" aria and not Frantz's, I asked Ray if I could sing Kleinzack for him.

Sure, no problem.

Ray's apartment also happened to be located in the same upper Manhattan neighborhood as Hebrew Tabernacle, two or three blocks to the south.

Hummm... If he assigns me a role, arranging rehearsal time will be a snap.

Over six feet tall, Ray's slim baby face belied his thinning hair. He wore a perpetual smile, exuding the Buddhism he studied and practiced. The day I arrived for my audition, he wore shabby dungarees with a short-sleeved flowery sports shirt. I thought I had taken a wrong turn somewhere along Broadway and arrived in Honolulu—and told him so.

He laughed and greeted me warmly and then offered me tea and a generous portion of a salad he was preparing. We talked about music, his friendship with Tom, and the city music scene in general. I inquired about the opera company, and the piece that grabbed me was that they intended to use a full orchestra, uncommon for amateur companies.

That'll be a first for me!

Eventually, we got down to singing. I was most impressed with his playing, about which he apologized—needlessly as far as I was concerned. I sang well because Ray made me feel relaxed and quite at home. The experience was more akin to singing for the heck of it, as Jim and I had done in Ocean Grove; it really didn't feel like an audition. When I finished Hoffmann's "Kleinzack" aria, Ray turned to me with what can only be described as a heavenly smile, and declared slowly and emphatically, "But Bob, you are Hoffmann."

I bit my lower lip, feeling my eyes moistening. I rarely received such affirmation—never from my father, or even my mother for that matter, never from a teacher or coach, and certainly never at an audition. I had imagined and hoped he would tell me that although I was too good for the smaller parts, he really needed a much bigger and more mature voice for Hoffmann, but that he would cast me as Franz. In my wildest fantasies I never anticipated what he had just said to me.

Recovered from the pleasant shock, my first thought was: Mme Ryss! Oh, my gosh. She'll tear my head off. "Tuu drah-MAH-tik for you!"

I told Ray about my situation, her reluctance to let me perform, but at the same time, all she had done for me. As we talked about it he insisted the part was just right for me, and that he hadn't heard a tenor who came even close to my level of singing. He really wanted me to sing this production with him.

So I accepted it. I'll figure something out.

I decided not to tell Mme Ryss. I learned the role and sang it totally without her, but with Rays' help and support, of course.

In the meantime, just as the rehearsals with Ray began, I auditioned for the Amato Opera Company in New York's Bowery. Tony Amato, founder, director, chief cook and bottle-washer, liked me so well that he offered me the role of Fenton in Verdi' Falstaff on the spot. "It's a brand new production," he explained. "We've never done this opera before, but you're going to love it. Classes start in two weeks."

To sing with Amato a new singer was required to take staging classes for the role. It was a two-way street: Tony charged each singer a nominal fee to keep the company going, and the singer learned staging that, according to Tony, would prepare you to sing the role at the Met. He was a great teacher; I have never begrudged him his fee.

When I told Mme Ryss that the Amato Opera Company had offered me the role of Fenton, well, that changed everything between us. That was the role for me, she declared.

Classes in Falstaff began in September of 1973 and I debuted with the Amato Opera Company on February 23, 1974. That February performance was followed by two more in that first season and again in September. I repeated Fenton in the seasons from 1974 through 1979, and again in 1983–1984. Tony used me quite often as a replacement for other tenors. I've lost count of my performances.

Bob, between the acts, in Fenton's costume behind the Amato Opera house.

Bob as Fenton, with Diane Heitner as Nanetta, in Verdi's Falstaff, Act 1
Live performance of March 16, 1974, Amato Opera Theater.

An entrance in my debut in Act II, Scene 2 was unforgettable.

Nannetta and I come onstage to uproarious pandemonium with Falstaff shouting complaints and throwing laundry all over the place. The ladies shouted back, insisting he hide from Ford, the man he offended, in a large laundry basket, but he is being obstreperous about it. I had never before seen the full action, as it had always been passed over in the classes and rehearsals I attended. When I came onstage that night, I unwittingly dropped character and started to watch what was going on. I laughed and missed my next musical entrance. Tony sang it for me from the pit as he conducted—and glared at me. That was not the last time he would sing an entrance for me.

Nannetta, also laughing, became disoriented. Tony gave us both the evil eye through the lights. I took Nannetta by the arm and quickly led her downstage left where we hid behind a screen. Once there we huddled together and snickered like a couple of school kids.

Another story from that unforgettable night concerns Act III, Scene 1, which contains the only aria for me in the opera, "Dal labro il canto estasiato vola" ("From my lips my ecstatic song is winging"). Providing a bit of a vocal challenge, the aria begins slowly with long legato lines requiring considerable breath control along with a very high tessitura—the technical word for hanging out in a particular range of the voice—adding to the difficulty, all of which I trained for by running and biking.

Dal labro is preceded by a languorous orchestral introduction. Tony used this music to drop a scrim of the large oak tree in two sections, one from above, and one from below. Once in place, it dominates center stage. The trunk scrim came up from a roller on the stage floor while the branches dropped as a scrim from above, the sections met halfway, taking only two to three seconds to accomplish. It appears to the audience to magically grow before their eyes. This stunning effect invariably brought applause, and I could hear murmurs of approval and astonishment as I awaited my entrance just off stage.

Having seen this scene from the house during rehearsals, I can tell you that the tree coming together made a sort of woo-oo-sh sound. But standing a few feet away, nervously awaiting my entrance, it sounded more like a crash.

In rehearsals, the tree was already in place. The first time I heard it was from standing near it backstage in this, my debut, and I nearly jumped out of my skin, instinctively raising my arms to protect my head, cringing for the impact—which never happened, of course. Just as quickly all was quiet again except for the soft brushing of the support ropes now relieved of their burden.

Once the tree is in place, I am supposed to enter in a dreamy state.

Relax, Robert. Calm down. It's okay. They applauded—not laughed. Think dreamy. Think Nannetta. Yeah, that's it, Nannetta. Well, here goes . . .

My first notes were to come as I kneel in a spotlight beside this wondrous tree. From backstage my knees were buckling, but I forced myself to step onstage. The tree was only a few feet ahead of me. Each step bolstered my courage, so by the time I knelt down I was ready to sing. I dare say my aria was well received—including a few bravos, actually.

Falstaff, being my first opera with Amato, has many fond memories, both of performances and colleagues with whom I sang. After 1984 my voice moved in the direction of heavier roles and I never returned to it.

After that first performance I felt my singing career was a YES!

But then I thought of Dad. I could hear his accusing voice ringing in my head, How much are you getting paid for all this effort of yours?

I cringed when I thought how much it was costing me, not earning a cent.

I could hear him smirking, I told you so…

On the other hand, not only did Mme Ryss encourage me and work with me on this opera, she also came to a performance on Sunday, September 22, 1974. She was eighty-one at the time and did not get around easily. Joan and I picked her up on our way to the theater from New Jersey and drove her home again. On the way home our car broke down on Fifty-Seventh Street. What a nightmare that dratted split engine hose turned out to be. She opted to take a taxi the rest of the way, while we waited for the tow truck for the long trek back to New Jersey.

Mme Ryss, enthralled with Tony's work in Falstaff, could not believe what he had accomplished in such a small theater. She knew what she was talking about because she had directed an opera company in South Africa for many years. Luminaries such as legendary baritone Lawrence Tibbett and the aforementioned mezzo, Jennie Tourel, sang with her company, along with many other opera stars.

"Vat he did vit dat tiny t'eater!" she exclaimed over and over in praise of Tony.

Things between Mme Ryss and me were just fine—and, she never knew about the Hoffmann.

Chapter 10

A Banner Year

1974

Nineteen seventy-four was a watershed year, both musically and personally. One month before my debut as Fenton in Falstaff, our first son, Robert Jr., "Rob," made his own debut on January 16. To be sure, I was thrilled with him, and felt honored to be present at his birth. On the other hand, suddenly, for the first time, Joan and I were no longer masters of our schedules. With everything revolving around this tiny new person, juggling my career at Scholastic and my ever-increasing singing commitments became a challenge that put a strain not only on my singing progress, but on our marriage as well. Joan began to feel deprived of my company. Nevertheless, we were determined to make it all work—somehow.

Despite all this, for the first time in my life I felt as though I was finally on my way to becoming the singer I wanted to be, not to mention now being a very proud papa. I felt both the Met and City Opera were coming within reach with the stage experience and expert coaching I was getting. But you always need a lucky break. Ask any singer who made it. Would I get one?

Working in New Jersey necessitated travel by car into Manhattan for rehearsals with Amato, who was downtown on the Bowery, and lessons with Mme Ryss, who lived uptown on West Seventy-Eighth Street; parking was always a challenge in both locations. The Hoffmann rehearsals began in upper Manhattan at Ray Fowler's apartment, but shifted to Edison, New Jersey, when staging rehearsals got underway. Just for some perspective, the trip from Bergenfield to Edison took an hour one way.

When performances or important rehearsals fell on a Friday evening, I had to hire a substitute to sing in the synagogue. If I had a Saturday matinee, I needed a sub for the Saturday morning services. Often for a Sunday afternoon performance, I engaged a sub for my church job.

Managing my schedule presented many challenges, not the least of which was trying to find time to spend with my new family. Later in the spring I juggled lessons and rehearsals between the Bronx Opera Company and the Middlesex Opera Company. The Hoffmann with Middlesex was scheduled in May, with rehearsals quite different from anything I had encountered.

Our stage director was Victoria Holder, who seemed to me like a Hoffmann scholar, providing all the lead singers with oodles of background material on the opera, drafts, and articles that she had researched on the life and stories of the actual, historical E. T. A. Hoffmann, plus additional material on each of the characters we were performing. She encouraged us to look up the various tales he had written that are alluded to in the opera. I don't know how the other singers reacted to all this required reading, but I loved it. In fact, I still have all my material on file, which I go back to every time I perform the opera.

The cast and chorus of this group turned out to be fond of partying, and they invited me to join them, much to my wife's disapproval. Foolishly, I fell in with them, thinking, "No problem, I can handle this."

When my friends insisted, "Come on, Bob," pulling me by the arm, I laughed and went along with them, not giving it a second thought. When I was in college I frowned on the party crowds. At this point in my life I felt I had missed out and wanted to make up for lost time. Looking back on it I later realized that acting like a teenager risked both my job at Scholastic and my voice, not to mention my marriage. Some nights were quite long, getting me home in the wee hours, which made getting up for work the next day quite a drag. But somehow I got through it all, and the performances went off reasonably well.

Adding to my burdens, I auditioned for and won the small role of a priest in Magic Flute with the Bronx Opera Company in April and May. Although Marlena Kleinman had advised me against singing small roles, every young singer in New York aspires to work with the Bronx Opera Company. They are the top of the opera minor leagues—if there were such a thing.

Founded in 1967 by Michael Spierman, the BOC offers two productions a year, one in the winter and another opera in the spring. They perform at Lehman College in the Bronx, at Hofstra University on Long Island, and at Hunter College in Manhattan. BOC has resources and staff that most small companies do not. They produce high-quality operas that get reviewed in major New York newspapers. BOC has been a stepping-stone for many a young singer to major houses. Michael assured me that this role was a good entrance into BOC, and that I had a future with them.

When I joined them in 1974, they performed at the Bronx High School of Science, at Lehman College in northwest Bronx, and at Hunter College in Manhattan. (Hofstra University came after my time.) Initial musical rehearsals were held at Michael's apartment in the Bronx with staging and orchestra rehearsals at the high school, which was nearby. My debut with the BOC on April 26, 1974, at the Bronx High School of Science Auditorium marked the beginning of a long and fruitful relationship with the company and with Michael, as well as the opportunity to work with a number of notable singers, stage directors, and conductors. I wish I could have told Dad, BOC pays its singers—modestly, but it's better than nothing! Michael once told me it was a matter of respect for his artists, even though the fee was but a token.

BOC, incidentally, is one of the few opera companies of the fifteen with which I sang that is still going strong.

The summer of '74, I auditioned for and landed the role of Camille in the Princeton Opera Association's summer production of Lehar's Merry Widow. By this time, after Rob's birth in January, Joan was singing again and joined me in this production, singing a small part. Rob was small enough that we took him with us everywhere. It was also a way of keeping the family together outside of home.

The audition for Camille took place at the studio of the conductor and music director of POA, Igor Chichagov. Igor had been the accompanist of the famous Italian-American soprano, Rosa Ponselle, whom Caruso championed into the Met. His studio at the Ansonia Hotel on Seventy-Third Street in the city was to become a kind of second home for me over the next seventeen years, as Igor became my principal repertoire coach who taught me most of my roles.

The performances of Merry Widow took place at the Open Air Theatre at Washington Crossing State Park in southwest New Jersey. I had never sung in the "open air" before, so this presented a challenge of a different sort. Outside you don't get the vocal reverberations from the walls, which help to focus the voice. In open air, your voice flies away from you with no sound coming back to judge how you're doing vocally.

I guess I did pretty well, though, considering Susan Sprague's review in the Thursday, September 5, 1974, edition of the Bucks County Courier Times:

> *Robert Mitchell singing the part of the Parisian Camille was the outstanding male voice in the show. His beautiful voice rang true on every note, …*

(Used by permission)

In September I sang another Fenton at Amato, followed by my first Tamino (Magic Flute) on Saturday, December 7, 1974. Of course, I had taken Tony's class for it, as I did for all fifteen of my roles at Amato. At Mannes, I had learned the role in German, but ironically, never performed it auf Deutsch. Tamino was easy enough to relearn in English for this production and was to become one of my favorite and oft-performed roles at Amato.

By this time, I knew not to mention roles to Mme Ryss that she thought out of my league. The opera community in which we moved was small enough that she might find out. If she did, she might throw me out. At best, she would have made my life miserable. Plus, I felt I owed her for the year of free lessons. At first I almost told her about Tamino because of my Fenton success, but stopped myself. She let me work on his first aria, a difficult piece with a high tessitura to sustain. In English it begins: "Oh, image, angel-like and fair, no mortal can with thee compare."

The first note starts in the middle range and jumps to a fairly high note on the next syllable, "O im-age…" The problem for me is the second note, on an ĭ sound. This vowel is between a pure "ee" sound and an "eh" sound, and has always bedeviled me, especially on high notes.

Mme Ryss quickly stopped me, "You pushed dat note."

I stopped and looked at her quizzically.

"Again," she commanded.

"Oh, ĭ – ĭ – ĭ ---m." She stopped me abruptly.

"You pushed dat note. It's na-ZAL," she said, pointing at my nose accusingly.

By this time I had learned not to argue with her. I took a deep breath and tried it again, and again, and again.

Growing angry, she pointed to my diaphragm and shouted, "You push your breat'."

I tried easing off my breath. That didn't work. I tried pressing harder on my breath.

Mysteriously—she accepted that. But I did the opposite of what she asked me to do. Not only did that frustrate me, but she seemed to accept different versions at different lessons. I could never come away from a lesson saying, "Oh, that's the problem!" because I had no idea what the problem was, nor worse, how to fix it. Her stock answer was, "Float dat note…"—whatever that meant. Well, I knew what she meant, but how to do it evaded me.

Despite all these difficulties, I sang the role quite successfully and often. Tamino did not ruin my voice. Sometimes I wondered why I continued my lessons with her.

One night during a Magic Flute performance I fell asleep onstage in the long opening scene in which I have fainted after fighting a large, ferocious serpent. Three ladies appear and kill the serpent before it gets me. The trio that follows seems endless, and I suppose I had not had enough sleep the night before, because I literally conked out. I could hear the three ladies singing in my subconscious. When they ended their trio and departed, the music stopped. Spoken dialogue was to begin with me—being alone on stage. I was supposed to wake up and say, "Where am I?" In the silence I fell deeper asleep.

Perhaps I was snoring because Tony, who was conducting that night, whispered, "Bob!" The Amato Theater was quite small and I was lying next to the footlights, actually close enough for him to reach up from the pit and clap me on the head. But Tony would not spoil a scene if he could help it.

I guess something in the stage surroundings—the dusty floor, the sets, the lights, or Tony's anxious voice—prompted my inner brain to signal my mouth to say my next line, "Where am I?" right on cue, or perhaps a little late. I said it, but I spoke out of my dream world more than in the show. For those few seconds of struggling to my feet, I had no idea where I was. It was like an out-of-body experience. What a wacky feeling. I still wonder if anyone in the audience noticed. I'm sure those seated close to the stage must have realized that something was not quite right. Did they think I was drunk? Or the opposite, that I was an actor totally engrossed in the role? By the time I got to my feet I came out of my stupor and continued as if nothing was wrong.

Another performance, of all nights to get sick, was the only occasion Joan and I were ever scheduled together in Flute. It was seldom enough that we sang together in opera productions, but it was far more seldom that I got sick enough to cancel. But to miss a performance with her left a big hole in both our singing careers.

In September I applied to the Opera School of Chicago, sponsored and operated by the Lyric Opera of Chicago. I received a letter announcing that I was to audition for them at Carnegie Hall in New York on October 8, 1974. I sang "Qual destino" ("Ah, mes amis") from Donizetti's Daughter of the Regiment.

I chose this aria because of a young Italian tenor who had captured critics and the public alike with his nine high-Cs in this very role—which, as opera lovers know, catapulted the young Luciano Pavarotti from a leading singer at the Met to a star overnight, soon to become a superstar. Everyone raved about his spectacular high-Cs in this aria, including me, and Mme Ryss herself, who raved so much about Pavarotti that I announced to her, "I can sing that."

She looked dubiously at me. "Bring it to me," she said.

I did and we worked on it. She was quite pleased, and for the first time I didn't get the "too dramatic" lecture, nor stopped so much for pushed notes. She also did not comment on the fact that I sang it in Italian. Even Pavarotti, the quintessential Italian tenor, sang it in French, the language in which Donizetti composed it. I had borrowed a score of the opera from the New York Public Library; the only copy they possessed was in Italian. I didn't know at the time that it was always given in French, so I learned it in Italian.

Years later a dear opera friend, David Schechter, questioned why I had recorded the aria in Italian. My first reply was that Donizetti is Italian. Dave pointed out that Donizetti composed it in French for the Paris Opera, and it's always given in French. I felt like a country bumpkin.

In the meantime I was selected to go to Chicago to the final auditions on the stage of the Lyric Opera on December 4, 1974. In my letter I had written the seven arias I had prepared especially for the auditions, with "Qual Destino" as the first. No one said anything about my singing it in Italian. Their letter had instructed me to be prepared to sing arias in various languages and moods, including something in English. Two were in English.

Walking on to the cavernous Chicago Lyric stage, I remembered the time I walked on to the stage of the old Met through a friend who worked there. So here I was in Chicago, my first trip to the "Windy City." My heart jumped for joy—and apprehension. As I walked across to center stage, I summoned every fiber of dignity and confidence to look out into an empty, dark, intimidating theater. Halfway back, there was a row of soft lights illuminating the desks of the audition listeners, one of whom I recognized: the much vaunted Carol Fox, the General Manager of Lyric Opera. My heart skipped a beat.

Carol Fox herself is listening to me?

I sang "Qual destino" first and Ms. Fox asked for a second aria. "Something in English," she said, explaining that much of the repertoire of the Opera School is in English. I offered the "Kleinzach" aria, which I had recently performed in English with the Middlesex Opera.

There was a long pause after I sang. An open door at the back of the auditorium leading to a lighted hall busily accommodated people bustling in and out. By and by, someone came through the door and marched directly towards the stage to retrieve me. The nattily attired woman motioned me to follow her. I had no idea we were destined for Ms. Fox's office. Once there, being escorted to her office made me feel very important indeed.

Ms. Fox welcomed me warmly. She commented how much she liked my singing and my artistry. "You've had excellent training," she said with a smile.

Then the mood changed to a more somber note. I thought, Uh-oh. She had noticed on my application that I was married and that we'd recently had a child. Moreover, she noticed that I had been working for Scholastic since 1968, all of which I acknowledged proudly with a big smile.

She then launched into a description of the program, which she emphasized was only a year in duration. I would receive a monthly stipend of $1,000.

My smile grew wider as she spoke. Great!

Then she started asking me questions: "Where will you live? You can't live in the student dorm with a family. You would have to get an apartment. Can you afford that and all your living expenses on $1,000 a month here in Chicago? It's expensive—like New York." It was clear she didn't think so.

My enthusiasm began to fizzle.

"What will you do at the end of the year's program? The chances of your getting into Lyric Opera are very slim indeed. This program is designed to ready you for regional houses, not major ones. Can you risk losing your career at Scholastic?"

I had not anticipated questions like this and had indeed been looking at this program through rose colored glasses—much as the character of Hoffmann in Act 1. My dream had been to float from this program right onto the Lyric Opera roster. My bubble burst all over my soul.

They promised to let us know by the first of the year. Their decision came much earlier, about two weeks later, expressing regret and offering me a chance to apply again next year. Really? I don't think so.

On December 29, 1974, I sang a recital at the Bronx Museum. By this time Michael Spierman (artistic director of the Bronx Opera) and I enjoyed a friendship, which for me was rare with a conductor. He liked my work well enough to arrange this recital, and he brought in one of the finest accompanists in the business, Myron McPherson, to work with me on this project.   December 29 happens to be Joan's birthday, so I am much obliged to her for recording this performance when we should have been out celebrating her birthday. She used our home Tandberg reel-to-reel tape recorder, the best such home machine available in the seventies, and caught my voice in its prime, with breath control like Pavarotti himself—it happened sometimes.

The space where I sang was an open area much like a European train station. There were folding chairs for the audience, which clanged occasionally as people came and went. Passersby wandered in and out and through the area, sometimes stopping to see what was going on, other times annoyed at the obstruction, throughout the concert. On the recording you can hear an occasional chair clang or scrape against the floor, the customary coughs, and even a jet plane flying over during the Handel piece (from the oratorio, Jephtha). The pilot chose a good time to pass: between the recitative and the aria. Myron smoothly paused for him to pass before we launched into the aria.

The first half of the program was inspired in part by Johnny's Jussi Björling LP record of his Carnegie Hall recital of September 24, 1955, the one I copped from him. The second half of my program was the entire Dichterliebe of Robert Schumann, which consists of twenty songs. Several selections from this work are also on YouTube.

Yes, 1974 was quite a year!

Okay, Dad, waddya think of me now? This has been a good year. Yes, ups and downs are part of the process. And don't give me that "where's the money" crap, because I'm building something here, a future, a career, a place in history. The money will follow, you'll see.

I didn't mention above that I had won a singing contest this year resulting in an appearance on the WGN radio program, "Opera Stars of Tomorrow." Wish you could have heard it.

Somebody will discover me, just you wait...

Chapter 11
Rodolfo, Middlesex, Opera Studio

1975-1976

The next year was not nearly as busy. I added the role of Hoffmann to my Amato repertoire on Saturday, May 22, 1975. Although singing the role in English with Middlesex in 1974 gave me a jump start on it, Tony's version was significantly different from Middlesex's. He rearranged a number of the scenes, which took some getting used to. In addition to my having to relearn much of the text in French, we also had to learn spoken English dialogue which Tony himself added to help the audience follow the more complicated scenes.

Starting in the late fall of 1974, I was already in rehearsal for Middlesex Opera's production of Puccini's La Boheme, being staged to celebrate the opening of Middlesex County College's new Performing Arts Center, also in May. When conductor Ray Fowler and stage director Vicky Holder from the 1974 Hoffmann were retained to lead this new production, they asked me to sing Rodolfo. This was the first time I was invited by an opera company to sing a particular role, instead of having to try out for a part. You can imagine how I felt—like a big-time star. It's one thing to be invited to audition, but to be invited to sing a role—well, that's a new ball game. Am I moving up in the singing world or what?

How 'bout them apples, Dad? …Will somebody discover me this time? It's so frustrating not to be noticed by the people that can help…

Singing Boheme in English, contrary to many opera lovers' strongly-held conviction, turned out to be rewarding. The translation remained faithful to the Italian text and was not as hard to sing as many singers complain. It also prepared me for another English production that came up unexpectedly the following year.

The college went all out to make this a gala affair by providing a full orchestra. I had sung with a full orchestra with the Bronx Opera, but in a small role. Singing Rodolfo with a full orchestra required some adjustments. I had to face forward at all times to prevent my voice from being lost in the wings. It was also important, as Mme Ryss used to say, "put an ice bag on your head!" She meant, "Don't panic! Don't push! Trust your voice" to carry over the orchestra. Pace yourself, I told myself, because Rodolfo is onstage for most of the four-act opera.

Speaking of Mme Ryss, I didn't tell her about this production, either. I didn't want to hear her verbal barrage again.

As to staging, I knew I might have to ignore or finesse some stage positions or movements in order to face out. No worries. Judy Nicosia was my Mimi, my angel. We helped each other shine, especially when the other was in the limelight.

Just before the last performance of Boheme, I stuck my head in the women's dressing room to tell Judy how much I enjoyed working with her. Seated in front of her makeup mirror, she noticed my uninvited head dangling by the door and turned around as I walked up behind her and intending to put my hands on her shoulders to say my thank yous in her ear.

Before I got there, she laid down her eyebrow pencil, turned to me and said loud enough for all to hear, "Bob, you are wonderful to work with, and the best tenor I have ever heard. You are going to have a major career—mark my words."

Deeply moved, I wanted to take her in my arms and kiss her—but I remembered my marriage vows. Besides, I didn't want to smear her makeup—or mine. Her generous words came to mind a few years later when I saw her name on the roster of City Opera.

After the first performance, the orchestra timpanist, Achilles "Archie" D'Amico, sought me backstage to tell me how impressed he was by my performance. He also told me that he was the percussionist in the orchestra of the New Jersey State Opera Company, and that he wanted to arrange an audition for me with Maestro Alfredo Silipigni, artistic director of NJSOC.

Am I being discovered?

I enthusiastically accepted his offer, but it took until the spring of 1976 to finally meet the maestro, after my stint with Opera Studio.

Maestro Silipigni was impressed enough with me to invite me to sing the tenor aria, "Recondita Armonia" from Tosca, for a fund-raising concert at the Paper Mill Playhouse, New Jersey's premiere regional theater in Millburn. My friend and fellow tenor from Opera Studio, Robert Van Valkenberg, also on the program, sang another Tosca aria, "E lucevan le Stelle."

Silipigni introduced both of us to the audience as rising young tenors who deserved to be heard. He went on to say that he would love to cast singers like the two waiting in the wings in the role of Cavaradossi, but you (the audience) would not come. In order to get you to come, he would have to cast Placido Domingo—or words to that effect. He went on to complain how much of his budget was spent engaging international singers when he would love to give young American singers like Bob and me a chance. I was proud of him for making such a courageous statement, but astonished that he scolded the very people he hoped would dip into their wallets.

Earlier at my audition with Silipigni, he offered me the part of Spoletta in the Tosca production in which Domingo was to star in the fall. Again, acting on the advice from our friends to not sing small parts, I turned him down.

Oh, Robert! Bad choice! Just think—you would have been onstage with Placido Domingo. What might have been…? Joan says let it go, but I keep kicking myself.

The year 1976 turned out to be much busier than 1975. In March I sang Rodolfo with Opera Studio. I vividly remember auditioning for Joseph "Joe" Bascetta in late 1975, responding to an announcement in Back Stage News, a newspaper source for auditions and theater calls. I had already performed Rodolfo in English with the Middlesex Opera the previous spring. At that time Joe lived in the West Seventies where I went to sing for him, surprised I would be singing in such a small basement apartment.

After we greeted one another, we got right down to business. Since I was auditioning for Rodolfo in La Boheme, I naturally was prepared to sing his big aria, "Che gelida manina."

Partway through the aria, Joe stops me.

Oh, no! Here comes the thanks-but-no-thanks brush-off.

Joe, a slight, wiry fellow, built like a dancer, with dark hair, intense dark eyes that sparkle when he smiles, saunters over to me with just such a smile and asks me what I'm singing about.

Remembering that humbling encounter with Singher a dozen years before, I begin to translate the aria for him.

Joe shakes his head, waves his hand in front of me, and exclaims, "No, no, I don't want a translation! I asked you, 'What are you singing about?'"

To my bewildered expression he responds, "Here, let me show you what I mean," and walks to a nearby doorway and calls a name down a staircase.

I'm surprised there's a room below the basement level. Up the stairs and into the room walks a lovely wisp of a girl with flowing, waist-length light-brown hair, pure white skin, and flashing blue eyes. The sight of her takes my breath away. Joe directs me to the couch and seats me close to her, placing her soft, lily-white hands in mine, gently positioning her head to look squarely and lovingly into my eyes. Pleased with the picture he has thus created, he leans over to me and whispers conspiratorially in my ear, "Just tell her who you are." He turns back to the pianist with a wink and a nod to start again.

I doubt I ever sang the aria as well as that second go-through. Indeed, the part was mine, alternating with Bob Van Valkenberg, who had already been selected for the other cast. I debuted with Opera Studio on March 18, 1976, at the Cubiculo Theater on West Fifty-First Street, known for its theater-in-the-round, and then sang it again two days later. Boheme, being an intimate opera, worked well in that venue. Certainly, the venue has a big impact on the performance.

Working on a traditional stage feels like working in two dimensions, but theater-in-the-round, with the audience all around you, feels more three-dimensional—and in that sense, more "real." You have to be aware of your back because it always faces some part of the audience, unlike traditional theater where you want your back away from the audience— usually. I felt enriched as an actor for having that unique experience, which I never encountered again in my singing career.

Something else happened in this production, quite unanticipated, and yet, always risky for stage characters who fall in love as part of the story. Judy James was my Mimi. She had lusciously dark auburn hair, very white skin, and soft brown eyes that entranced me. In fact, when I sang with either my wife or her, I changed the line "ma di quegl'occhi azzuri allo splendor" (but at the splendor of those blue eyes) to "ma di quegl'occhi bruno allo splendor" (but at the splendor of those brown eyes). Even Sue Peters, our exacting musical director, never said a word about my little change to Giacosa and Illica's libretto.

Judy and I had a rapport, a chemistry that made the role of Rodolfo very special. Thinking about it today reminds me that she helped shape my understanding of Rodolfo—and even of myself.

When Judy (Mimi) sings the "Farewell" in Act 3, I (Rodolfo) cannot bear to face her. During this aria she offers to give me back the bonnet, as a keepsake, I had bought her in Act 2. I turn away, suppressing tears—this was our last performance in this production, and we both believed it was our last performance together—forever.

Tears streamed down her cheeks. The sight of them chokes me up, making it difficult to sing. Her farewell aria ends to warm applause. The conductor signals me to continue with my next line, without orchestra, "Then it is really finished!" I choke on the words…

Love onstage is one thing; offstage is quite another matter. Even though working full-time for Scholastic, I found ways to spend time with her. Sometimes we worked our scenes at her home in Brooklyn, mostly when her husband was there. Occasionally we had lunch or coffee alone together in the city.

One evening, Judy and her husband went out to dinner with Joan and me. It was a cold night; Judy wore a long, flowing overcoat with a fur-lined hood. I don't know what possessed me, but as we left the restaurant I paused under a streetlight that glowed with soft yellow light, and turned her to frame her face in her hood with the moon-like light, and sang "O soave fanciulla" (the last scene of Act 1 in which we declare our love for one another) softly to her. For me this moment caught the quintessential picture of Mimi and Rodolfo together. The blur between Mimi and Rodolfo and Judy and Bob was obvious to everyone around us.

Needless to say, this little scene upset both our spouses, and I deeply regret all the pain I caused Joan through this production. She and I had sung La Boheme together, and we dreamed of making a career of operas like this. Moreover, in our wedding album there is a photo of the two of us dancing with the words and music of "O soave fanciulla" in the background. So my attention to Judy was doubly agonizing for her and now has become a penance for me.

Oh, the foolishness of youth! Just as love in the great classic stories can inspire us to dream of ideal love, we performers can experience these illusive fantasies, if just for a moment, onstage. Sometimes when a partner senses your feelings are real, she responds. I read a book on acting called,

Acting Is Believing. Its thesis was that only if you totally commit and immerse yourself in your character can you become believable onstage. The danger of these raw emotions spilling offstage is ever present. It happens to movie stars as we see in the press continuously—it happens to us as well.

Emotionally as well as physically, Judy always kept me at arm's length. I was never sure of her feelings for me, any more than I was certain of my own feelings for her…

"…Then it is really finished…" Mimi and Rodolfo realize their tempestuous love affair cannot last, but they decide to stay together through the cold winter months until spring arrives. At the end of the scene we walk offstage arm in arm, promising each other we will part "in the season of flowers," though our hearts ache at the thought of parting at all. Puccini's poignant music agrees…

For theater-in-the-round, we would have had to walk out of the theater to exit since there is no backstage. There isn't enough music to allow for that, so the stage crew had set up two screens at the edge of the stage for us to hide after we stop singing for the final couple of seconds.

When we arrive at the screen, every light in the theater blacks out for the few seconds until that last chord. As we squeeze behind the screens, I take her in my arms…

In past performances, as I held her loosely in my arms, we usually whispered or giggled something like, "Thank God that's over!" However, this night, neither of us was in a giggling mood…

…The instant the lights go out, she returns my passionate embrace, her lips find mine, and we kiss as lovers parting for the last time.

When the lights came back on for curtain calls, she quickly disengaged from me and walked out to receive the applause as though nothing had happened. I stood there mesmerized by our first and only kiss, savoring the taste of her lips on mine. As the applause grew, she looked back at me, quite unaware that her lipstick was smeared from her nose to her chin, and with a huge smile, motioned me to come out.

Seeing I was stuck to the spot, she skipped lightly back, grabbed my hand, and pulled me onstage to accept my share of the ovation. Smiling first to the audience to acknowledge their applause, I then turned to acknowledge Judy. I noticed her mussed makeup, and reached up and gently began to wipe away the unsightly smudges. The audience cheered as if they knew about the secret kiss from the beginning. Hand in hand, we acknowledged their gleeful enthusiasm.

I have no recollection what happened after that, not even the last act. I guess for me, at least, it all ended right there.

Judy and I sang together again, the Act 1 love duet from Boheme in the Lincoln Center Band Shell the following summer, and later that fall we collaborated in Opera Studio's production of Carlisle Floyd's Susannah, she in the title role, and I as her brother Sam. After that production I never saw her again. A year or so later she and her husband moved to the Midwest where he won a much sought-after professorship. I know she wanted to have a family; I can only hope her dream was fulfilled as it was for Joan and me.

This production of La Boheme was unique in many ways, not the least of which was working with Joe Bascetta, one of the highlights of my career. He's an exciting talent as well as a gifted teacher. I had hoped that Opera Studio would become a regional company—if not a major one—and I a major player over the course of time. My abiding regret was that after the four productions I sang with him (Boheme, Il Tabarro, Susannah and Crucible), Joe moved away from New York and Opera Studio was dissolved. (Joe was surprised to learn the name he created for us, "Opera Studio," is now being used by another New York director as of this writing.) Joe went on to become an acclaimed international director and teacher. He's currently the Artistic Director of the Fresno Grand Opera in Fresno, California.

Chapter 12
The Next Decade to Opera Classics

1977 to 1987

As the years trudged on, I progressed vocally and built repertoire as much as I could. I worked very hard to get an agent, sometimes through auditioning, sometimes through networking, and more often through personal contacts. Most agents, however, were not interested in inexperienced singers.

In addition I wrote to regional companies, offering to sing the roles I knew and had performed, often numerous times. But with a full-time job at Scholastic, how could I commit to work for them without giving up my career? It was a catch-22.

Joan and I occasionally dreamed about going back to Germany to try our "luck" (as they say) singing over there. But Rob was growing, and we had a mortgage to pay. With my career at Scholastic solidly on track, we knew we could not risk our jobs to further our singing aspirations. Joan had pulled back from the idea of a career, but I never wavered in my determination. Was it to prove Dad wrong? That may have been a piece of it, but I also yearned for the recognition of singing lead roles with companies recognized by the opera press.

The test I set up for myself to qualify as a professional singer was to be able to support my family through singing. In my heart I knew I was a "pro" as far as talent and ability were concerned. Singing as an amateur, which is what I was doing, didn't get the job done, even though I loved every minute of being onstage—no matter what the venue.

I continued to sing Fenton, Tamino and Alfredo at Amato. I sang Alfredo with another small company as well, the Manhattan Singers. I added Rodolfo to my Amato repertoire, along with Pinkerton and several more Verdi roles, Riccardo in Oberto, Manrico in Trovatore, Radames in Aïda, and Gustavo in Ballo. I also took on several interesting, lesser known roles with other companies, adding to my portfolio, making me more attractive to agents, regional houses, and major houses. Nevertheless, without the crucial break, I was going nowhere.

Meanwhile, back at the Amato Opera, Rodolfo had become a staple, meaning that every time Tony scheduled La Boheme, I got to sing it. Sometimes things didn't go as planned; one night, when I was about to offer Mimi a drink during a performance, I found myself without wine glasses nor the wine decanter.

Towards the end of the first act Mimi had just knocked on my door asking to relight her candle which had blown out in the drafty hallway. It was too dark to see the way to her apartment on the floor above. Even as she entered I could see she was unwell. And sure enough, muttering, "My breath...those stairs..." (translated from Italian) she keeled over. I caught her before she hit the floor and helped her into my beat-up easy chair. As soon as she recovered, I was to offer her some wine.

The decanter and glasses were supposed to be preset on the table at center stage. I was to pick up a glass and pour her some wine on the words "un po' di vino" (a little wine). Much to my horror, neither glass nor decanter was where they were supposed to be. She, now sitting with her back to the audience, looked at me with a childish gleam in her eye as if to say, "Now what are you going to do?" Abandoning the rehearsed staging, I smiled and held up a "just-a-minute" finger. Without missing a note, I looked around the stage and spotted the missing articles on an upstage cabinet—where they didn't belong.

I've got to talk to that stage manager!

Still following my own spur-of-the-moment staging, I casually sauntered upstage to retrieve them, much to her surprise and delight. She could hardly keep from giggling at my dilemma. Would I make it back in time for the "un po' di vino" line?

Not quite: I delivered it and poured the wine as I returned to her.

OK Mimi, it's time to get back in character...

From that night forward I never relied on a stage manager to have my props in place. I was the one out there with egg on my face, not him or her. So I always toured every stage on which I sang to make sure all my props were in place before the overture began.

Another night my Mimi was none other than Sally Amato, Tony's wife and opera partner, who sang under her maiden name of Serafina Bellantoni. Despite the many hats she wore backstage, including the lights and making costumes, she found time to don her own costume and makeup. The muse that calls us singers to the stage was no stranger to Sally.

She was New York City tough, and yet, underneath that street-wise exterior lurked the proverbial heart of gold. Most of the time she treated me like a star, that is, when she wasn't teasing me, or chiding me about my weight, especially with respect to our costumes—which she herself made. A stalwart tenor with whom I shared many roles and costumes, Vinnie Titone and I both took it on the chin about bursting costume seams. Sally made the Rodolfo costumes to fit all her tenors—or else.

Another sign of age was my receding hairline. I usually penciled it in. It wasn't until I saw a video of an Amato Hoffmann that I noticed the shining spot on the back of my head as I walked up stage. I was also getting bald in the back. How deflating!

This Boheme story doesn't involve costumes or makeup, but took place in the final scene where once again the bohemians had gathered in Rodolfo's room. Musetta interrupted a mock sword fight among the guys to ask for help with Mimi. "She's so sick she can't manage the stairs," she declared anxiously. Rodolfo and Marcello quickly rushed offstage to assist Mimi up the stairs, then guided her to the bed that she and Rodolfo shared in happier days.

At the end of this scene—and the opera—she died, unbeknownst to Rodolfo, who was talking quietly to Musetta across the room, each assuring the other that Mimi would make it. But suddenly he noticed the hushed conversation in the room had stopped.

"What's wrong?" he asked no one in particular.

Marcello rushed over to him, embraced him with a heart-felt, "Coraggio!" ("Courage!")

Grief-stricken and calling her name, Rodolfo threw himself over her body, weeping uncontrollably.

With my usual passion, I threw myself into this scene, but this time, throwing myself was too much for the bed, and the whole kit and caboodle, Mimi and Rodolfo included, crashed nosily to the floor. At first I tried surreptitiously to pick the bed up, but no way. Then I tried to make it look as though this was the way it was supposed to be—rather silly to try, really. What could I do?

You can't fool an audience. They began to titter, then looked at one another, and finally broke into unabashed laughter. Needless to say, it ruined the scene and spoiled the mood of the opera. Monty Python had slipped in unnoticed.

Backstage afterward was quite a different matter. Though she only came up to my shoulders, her furious finger in my face cut me down to her size. How could I ruin her death scene so callously? Did I hear the audience? We were a laughing stock…and on it went.

Tony stood by rather placidly, not saying a word.

Perhaps he realized, as I did, that covering an old, aluminum chaise lounge with tons of pillows and blankets to pass for a bed was a disaster waiting to happen, knowing that the weight of a tenor landing atop a soprano, well…

In the midst of all my singing engagements, my eight-to-four job at Scholastic, and singing in church and synagogue every weekend, our second son Randy staged his well anticipated debut at precisely 9:23 p.m. on September 3, 1979, weighing in at six pounds and seven ounces. After a few minor complications, Joan was soon up and about to join me in loving and taking care of our second little guy. Unlike when Rob was born, Joan's complications kept her out of circulation for a while. She complained that for some reason her breath control was never the same after Randy came through the channel. The mystery of it was that Rob caused her no such problem.

Rob, now five, was delighted with his new brother—but only because Randy was a boy. If he had been a girl, Rob had made it absolutely clear to Joan that she was to "send it back."

Taking care of two little ones complicated our calendar. Certain activities had to go and others were cut back, but with the help of Joan's parents, ever eager to sit with the boys, we managed quite well. For example, singing at Hebrew Tabernacle suddenly became a priority because we needed the additional income. When Rob was the only one to be looked after, we used to take him along, much to the delight of Cantor Ehrenberg, our boss. But we couldn't push our luck with two.

Joan's parents to the rescue: they happily invited the two little guys to stay Friday nights and Saturday mornings. Fortunately their house was near the George Washington Bridge, so we dropped them off on the way to the synagogue and picked them up after the Saturday morning service, usually around lunchtime. A win-win for all of us, especially the boys, who loved "sleeping over" at Grandma's, not to mention her great cooking.

"You're a good cooker, Grandma,"

It was also a win-win for Joan and me because we now had Friday nights and Saturday mornings to ourselves. Well, not exactly to ourselves. We had to sing at Hebrew Tabernacle, but we had the evening together traveling back and forth into Manhattan, plus we enjoyed our singing colleagues at the synagogue. Occasionally we would meet them for dinner, or go out afterward for coffee. Friday nights and Saturday mornings became a respite from the frenetic work week. Plus, we enjoyed the time for just the two of us...alone in the house for an entire night...hmm...

Later in September I sang for the first and only time the title role of Tito (Titus) in Mozart's La Clemenza di Tito with the Bel Canto Opera in New York. A year later I sang with Bel Canto again in the role of Tsar Berendey in Rimski-Korsakov's The Snow Maiden. Both operas were conducted by my longtime coach, Igor Chichagov.

Of Snow Maiden critic Peter Davis of the New York Times wrote that the lead soprano Marilynne Bird and I "stood out as the chief pleasures of the evening." Did that review have them banging at my door? Are you kidding, Robert?

In May of 1980 I sang Sam Polk (Susannah) with the Bronx Opera Company (BOC), a role I had made my own with Opera Studio. When I auditioned for the part, both Michael Spierman and stage director Nick Muni were there to hear the auditions at the Hunter College Theater in Manhattan.

I had come up with a great idea for this audition. Because of singing Sam with Opera Studio, plus my costume for OS was nothing more than my own work clothes, I decided to wear them to the Bronx audition. I had my walking stick, boots, and even wore a touch of makeup. Instead of just standing and singing, I also planned to act out the entire scene with an imaginary Susannah. I had an open gym floor to work with, so I thought, What have I got to lose? Go for it!

Hey, it worked! When I finished, Nick jumped to his feet shouting, "Bravo!" He not only was impressed with my performance, but my coming to the audition in costume knocked his socks off. He was also impressed how well I created the aura of Susannah's presence.

"You grabbed my attention and held it all the way. Great job, Bob!"

They hired me on the spot, something that never happened at a BOC audition. In all my years with them, there were always call-backs.

Nick, Michael and I worked together like a dream team. By this time Michael and I had two productions under our belts, my "legendary" Bronx Museum recital, plus an appearance with the Bronx Symphony Orchestra, Michael conducting, so he knew my work well. Nick became a third artistic partner with whom we, along with the entire cast, created a really fine show.

He taught me a lot about acting, movement, and stage craft in general. I am forever in his debt. A few years later Nicholas went on to an international career.

Times reviewer, Peter Davis, if not so exuberant as in Snow Maiden, commented that my performance made a "commendable contribution." Not bad, really, for a character that everyone forgets by the end of the opera. Maybe that's why nobody noticed me in this part, either?

In the lesser-known-roles department, May 1982, I added Eisenstein in J. Strauss' operetta, Die Fledermaus, to my repertoire with the Jersey Lyric Opera Company, my only production with them. It was rare for me to not be invited back, but sometimes singers and conductors don't hit it off. This was the only time in my career this happened to me. I did not like the way he treated certain singers, especially me, as if we were stray cats. I got in his face about it and told him we deserved better than that. He strongly resented being corrected, egotistical so-and-so that he was.

Normally they would have fired me, but he did not want to embarrass the lead soprano, a close friend of his, who had recommended me in the first place. She worked very hard to keep peace at rehearsals. I really don't know what his problem was. As they say, bad things happen sometimes.

Fledermaus is a very funny opera, but internal conflict can take the "funny" out of any scene. Both the conductor and I knew that, so we hunkered down to do the best professional job we could. As it turned out, audiences loved the show. No critics this time. No agents either.

November of 1983 saw me in the role of Radames in Verdi's Aïda at Amato. Some said it was a stretch for me—"too dramatic," but I managed it quite well. I sang it a number of times that season, and a few years later when Tony produced it again.

Despite the Fledermaus bump in my career, I was always a very conscientious, dependable performer. Most of the time, companies invited me back to sing. Not only did I know my part well, I never missed a stage entrance in any opera… wait a minute…except in Aida, my one, disastrous exception…which occurred one night in the Nile scene (Act III, Scene I).

There are a couple of long scenes that precede my entrance, so I had plenty of time—I thought! At Amato we normally waited backstage where we could hear what was happening onstage. But in Aïda, because of the large cast of singers and dancers, we principals had to wait in an upstairs loft where sets and costumes were normally stored. The sets and costumes had been moved elsewhere to accommodate us. From there, nothing could be heard from the stage.

To offset this problem, Tony rigged a sound system so we could hear what was happening onstage. In addition, he appointed a stage hand to cue us when it was time to go on. His sound system could have been improved with the use of a couple of cans connected by a string. As it was, most of what we heard through the speaker was noise that crackled in and out and sometimes disappeared. Turned up so that we could actually hear the music, an annoying speaker buzz set my teeth on edge. I tried to tune it out in order to study my score. Also, I wasn't concerned about missing my entrance because I knew the special stage assistant would call me.

I'm sitting upstairs here studying my score. My next entrance has several difficult and unfamiliar Italian words, along with some tricky musical entrances. At one point I turn the blasted speaker up to hear where they were onstage. Amonasro's words "Revedrai le foreste imbalsamate" hiss through the speakers.

Plenty of time. Back to the score.

Seems like only seconds have gone by when suddenly I hear Maestro Amato singing my entrance music. Horrified, I say to myself, How in the world did I miss that?

My mind racing, I jump to my feet and am aghast I'm the only person left in the loft.

Where'd everybody go? Where's the blasted stage person to cue me? I'm the lead tenor, for heaven's sake! Good Lord, now what am I gonna do?

I race down the steps two at a time, almost falling by catching the heel of my clumsy, ill-fitting stage shoes on the steps, and frantically catch the railing to prevent a disastrous tumble—this happens twice, drat it.

I'm to enter from the back of the theater and walk down the center aisle and up the left stairs to join Aïda onstage. We have some of the most romantic music of the opera coming up. But by the time I get downstairs, Tony is singing two pages further along... I should be onstage now! How did they get to this place so fast?

As I stand just outside the door of the auditorium, trying to decide what to do, my voice of reason takes over from my voice of panic: Calm down, Robert. Just go out there as if this is exactly what's supposed to happen.

Mustering every scrap of dignity I can, I stroll down the center aisle as if Tony had staged it this way. At the next pause in my music, I pick up the next line from Tony. Hearing me behind him, he immediately stops singing, but glares at me as I pass by him on the way to the stage. Our eyes meet for an instant.

"Where the hell were you?" they scream. I look away, otherwise I'd feel as if I needed to stop and explain to him what happened. The show must keep going...

Tony's anger is a walk in the park compared to Aïda as she watches me climb the steps to the stage, her face contorted with rage. I smile in character as if nothing's amiss. My next line is, "You will be the garland of my glory and we will live happily in eternity" (in Italian of course).

Her eyes shriek, "Yeah, right! You haven't got a prayer, Buster!"

Her next lines ooze sarcasm about what she suspects is going on between her rival, Amneris, and me, none of it true, by the way. In character, I try to convince her of my innocence. But her fury about the embarrassment of being left alone on stage singing with the conductor actually plays well for the scene. In the end we unwittingly make this scene incredibly effective, resulting in a rousing ovation from the audience.

Perhaps some of the applause is sarcasm for my foul-up—which knowledgeable opera goers couldn't miss. Later backstage, well, here we go again! Tony and Sally, not to mention the soprano, jump all over me.

My only consolation: the stage person who missed my entrance also has to deal with both Tony's and Sally's wrath.

Despite this notable glitch, Tony continued to use me. From 1984 through 1986 I repeated my signature roles—Rodolfo, Hoffmann, Alfredo, Tamino, and Pinkerton—now including Radames. I also added

Faust in 1985 and Don José in Bizet's Carmen in 1986, all at Amato (see listings of repertoire).

By the mid-eighties I was coaching with Linda Hall (today an Assistant Conductor at the Met), who decided I should study with a tenor for a change. "I have just the one for you," she declared, and sent me to Giovanni Consiglio, a dramatic tenor well known and well regarded in regional opera circles. Giovanni had a voice like a cross between Franco Corelli and Mario del Monaco. His voice intimidated me, but he was an affable and gentle teacher.

In the early spring of 1986, Giovanni casually mentioned in a lesson that his company, Opera Classics of New Jersey, "We plan-a production of Madama Butterfly for January next-a year."

My first thought was, Why is he telling me this? Does he want me to sing Pinkerton? To this day I'm not sure why he dropped this tantalizing tidbit before me, but trying to suppress my excitement at the prospect of (maybe) singing Pinkerton, I promptly said, "You know, I've sung Pinkerton many times [a lie in terms of full productions, but I had sung the principal music in concert often enough] I love that role." But when he didn't ask me, I asked him.

"We only use-a professional artists," he responded, with an emphasis on "professional."

That punched a hole in my balloon.

As the weeks wore on, I couldn't stop myself from dropping hints about how much I loved the role of Pinkerton. One day he said, "I sing-a Pinkerton myself-a."

I despaired, assuming the subject was now closed.

A few more weeks went by.

Then at another lesson he announced, "I wanna you to sing-a Pinkerton," but added with a finger pointed at me, "You cannot-a maik-a meestake, or Maestro [Anton] Coppola weel t'row you out!" Those ominous words haunted me throughout the entire production.

Ignoring them at the time, I could barely keep from jumping up and down and giving him a big hug. That's what I felt like doing, anyway. He didn't miss the excitement in my eyes and tone of voice when I thanked him. He smiled and said he wanted to give me this opportunity.

"Maybe somebody hear you," he said, shrugging a shoulder.

THIS IS IT, the beginning of a major career for me! Giovanni'll see to that!

I knew deep down that someone would hear me, someone who could help me, whether an agent, an impresario, or someone willing to back me. The way Giovanni had said, "Maybe somebody hear you," with a twinkle in his eye, I was sure he would see to it that somebody would hear me.

The big event was planned for January 31, 1987. It was certainly the most significant production in my singing career up to that point. I was the only singer in the cast who was not from the Met or City Opera. The Orrie de Nooyer Auditorium in Hackensack, New Jersey, was an immense theater and an important venue for musicians, singers and theater people. Also, because Opera Classics was an important regional company, I believed singing with them would make up for my gaff in rejecting the opportunity to sing a small part with the New Jersey State Opera.

This time I was singing a leading role; that makes all the difference.

I tried gallantly to convince myself, but, as the days wore on, one day I would surge with confidence, the next, I'd lapse into doubt. In hindsight I can see that I put enormous stress on myself over this production. "I have to sing well," I kept telling myself.

Contrary to my expectation, Giovanni made no attempt to alleviate my anxieties. He, in fact, added to them. A week or two before the performance he told me that my fee was to be $150.

Some years prior there was a professional singer who subbed at Hebrew Tabernacle—he sang with City Opera Chorus, and, in fact, was singing in this production. He became his own agent by disguising his voice over the phone and using a different name. He always told me, "Bob, never accept low fees, even if the company is giving you a break to sing." I believed him.

So I told Giovanni I thought the fee was a bit low. "Could you please see your way clear to give me more? Traveling back and forth into the city is expensive…"

In a flash he became an inferno of wrath, his thundering voice berating me like a child, telling me I was a "nobody" and was lucky beyond my station to appear with OCNJ. He reminded me that we had to exaggerate my bio because I had never "done anything important." All the singers in the cast were from either City Opera or the Met, he reminded me. "Who do you tink you are? You shoo'd be grateful for dis opportunity…" and on his tirade went. "You have no stage experience…

You sang this only at Amato? You tink Amato counts for some-ting? Hah! Eet's no-ting. He don't even have an orchestra…" And on and on it went. He concluded by saying he should take the role back, but it was too late for him to step in. "I don know you stagin'," he grumbled.

I felt reduced to a germ and wanted to disappear into the rug.

Our relationship was never the same after that, despite my earnest apologies. His demeaning remarks devastated me and truly compounded my performance jitters.

Even so, we began serious work on the role. He even brought me together with soprano Jolanta Rajewska, another of his students who was to sing Butterfly (Cio-Cio-San). We came to each other's lessons on several occasions to work on our scenes together with Giovanni.

Soon it was time to start the rehearsals, first with the other principals, and later, with the entire company. The company rehearsals began in a large hall near the Lincoln Center complex. I had studied and worked feverishly to re-memorize my part. I did not want to make that dreaded, fatal meestake. Not only did I not want to embarrass myself, I didn't want to get "t'rown out." I knew that would end any hope of a career.

The first staging rehearsals for blocking—the process of laying out stage positions and action for everyone—the opera came and went. I didn't get fired, so all was well with the world—for now.

Although he was already well known in the field, I have no recollection of the stage director, Franco Gentilesca. I became chummy, however, with prominent mezzo-soprano Leonore Lanzillotti, who sang Suzuki. She went out of her way to make me feel at ease by telling me that she too had sung at Amato. She told me that she had also graduated from Mannes and had sung at City Opera for several seasons. Well-known among the regional opera houses and musical theaters across the land, she became my bulwark and refuge. After what I had gone through—and put myself through, she was truly a God-send.

Knowing she and I shared artistic roots made me feel like part of the team at last.

One of the Met singers was up-and-coming Met baritone, Vernon Hartman, our Sharpless. Vern was a great guy and he too was supportive and helpful.

Others in the cast were busy trying to impress me with their importance, mostly the chorus people. Even they were City Opera or Met people. Some of them looked at me as if to say, "Who in blazes are you to be cast as Pinkerton? We expected to see somebody we know." They probably complained about it among themselves.

I'll never forget the first orchestral rehearsal with Maestro Anton Coppola, a well-known and respected regional conductor, a man who stood as straight as the proverbial arrow, with his gray mane crowning him like royalty. He always appeared dressed to the nines at rehearsals, trousers sharply pressed. The first orchestral rehearsals took place in a large hall on Broadway, probably built back in the twenties, up the street from Lincoln Center. The hall appeared to me as if it were more comfortable for banquets or dancing classes. It surprised me that we did not rehearse at Lincoln Center itself, or perhaps in a basement orchestral room at the Met. The concrete floor was painted and had metal pillars spaced strategically around the room, a hazard for dancers. No stage. When I entered the room for the first time, I noticed how the light streaming through windows along the top of the walls dappled the floor below.

Orchestra members and cast mingled; those who had worked together previously greeted each other and fell into conversation. Instrumentalists fussed over their instruments. Singers hummed to warm up as they looked for friends, while official-looking people scurried back and forth making last-minute adjustments to lights, music stands, and chairs. The room buzzed and crackled with chattering voices, instruments warming up, and people trying to talk over the din. I stood just inside the door, trying to take it all in, not knowing what to do or where to go. I looked for Leonore, Giovanni or Jolanta, the only people I knew, but to no avail.

Suddenly I turned and noticed Maestro Coppola standing somewhat in back of me to my left. I had never met him, but I knew instinctively who he was. Ignoring me and greeting no one, he cast bright eyes around the room like a robot sizing up the job ahead of him. No podium had been provided for him, so perhaps he was considering his options.

I thought to introduce myself, but as I turned to step toward him, he quickly passed me as if to prevent the encounter, and advanced across the room, adroitly carving himself an aisle through the not-so-orderly orchestra chairs. When he arrived at front and center where I supposed he imagined the podium should be, he turned on his heel and faced the room with a withering expression, somehow instantly silencing the room.

Like school children when the bell rings, orchestra members interrupted their conversations in mid-syllable and scrambled to find their places. Once seated, they maneuvered their music chairs and music stands for playing.

Singers, suddenly mute, ringed themselves around the back edge of the orchestra and opened their scores. Maestro Coppola ordered the chorus members to stand to his right, principals to his left. I joined them wondering if I truly belonged here, but acting as if I did.

Without another word he raised his hands (no baton), looked to his left, and leaned towards the violins which begin the opera, waited no longer than two seconds so they could get their instruments in place, and forthwith cast his right hand down like a gauntlet.

What amazed me was that without a preparatory beat, the strings followed him precisely in their opening flurry. He conducted the entire opera from memory, never budging from his spot until the end of Act 1, rather a long time. I don't recall him stopping at all on that first run-through. He kept mental notes on everything—that became apparent in subsequent rehearsals. He reminded me of old footage I had seen of Toscanini. I could easily imagine him throwing his baton à la the legendary maestro at a musician who botched something—except that Maestro Coppola used no baton for rehearsals. He did in performance, however. Actually, I was glad he had nothing in his hand he could throw at me.

I wanted to sing my part from memory, but my nerves wouldn't let me, so I furtively opened my score. Actually, as I looked up, I noticed everyone else opened theirs as well, so I took comfort in that. In a later rehearsal he ordered us to leave our scores aside. Panic set in; I really had to fight myself to get "off score," as we singers call it, and managed to do so in short order despite my nerves.

After surviving all the rehearsals without incident, in the performance itself there was a glitch that really threw me for a loop. It happened in the first scene of Act 1 in my scene with Sharpless. I was in the course of explaining to Sharpless the terms of the house I had rented for Cio-Cio-San and me. A certain line is to be preceded by a solo bassoon. It was a very tricky entrance because the bassoon line was very fast and I had to come in exactly so that both Sharpless and I could stay together with the orchestra. We never had a problem with this entrance in rehearsal and

Maestro Coppola had assured me beforehand that he would cue me. Good!

When I looked down at him for the promised cue, he was bending down to his right, angrily gesticulating at someone in the orchestra. I was horrified. What happened? I didn't know what to do. All this happened in the split of a second. My instincts—the show must go on—kicked in. Since Vern had already given me my previous cue, I counted the beat and a half and sang my next line. Maestro suddenly looked up at me and held up his left hand like a traffic cop to stop singing.

But this is the middle of my line. Why is he stopping me? What did I do wrong?

A second or two later, Maestro pointed a finger at me to resume the rest of my line. Fortunately I remembered where I was and came in on his cue. I knew something strange had happened but had no idea what. I thought I had made the "t'row-me-out" mistake, but then I realized, it's a little late for that now. What in blazes just happened?

As soon as the act was over, I sought Maestro backstage to ask him. At first he had no idea what I was talking about. When I described the place, he chuckled, "Oh, that! It wasn't you. It was the damned bassoonist who didn't come in. You were fine! The problem was that he started playing a measure late, so I had to hold you up for a measure, that's all. But it was certainly no fault of yours. It all worked out fine." And he scurried away.

I stood there for a moment not sure whether to be relieved or not. I watched him rushing down the hall and finally shrugged my shoulders at myself. So much for my fatal meestake! All that worrying for nothing!

I must have reverted to my teenage relationship with Dad from Giovanni's remonstration at the beginning, which intimidated me all through this production, so much so that immediately after the performance I came down with pneumonia. I had invested all my future hopes for a career in this one opportunity. As a result of the pressure I put on myself I was out of work from Scholastic for three weeks, and came within a cat's whisker of being hospitalized.

All that with no reviews, no agent, no impresario, no rich backer.

My coach, Linda Hall, sympathizing with this turn of events in my relationship with Giovanni, and quite aware that no one important had heard my Pinkerton, decided to send me to another teacher, a Met baritone friend of hers.

A different incident, but also in the so-close-yet-so-far-away department, happened one year later around this same time. Tony assigned me a Pinkerton in Puccini's Madama Butterfly. The show opened on a Friday night; I was to sing the second night, Saturday. Since I had already taken the classes for the role a couple of years prior, and had performed the role several times, the SOP for repeat performances was to attend as many rehearsals as you need to brush up the staging. (You were on your own for the music.)

In this instance, since I was singing the second night, there was only one rehearsal prior to mine, so I figured I had best get down to Amato's to see it.

When I walk in, I'm surprised to see a tenor already onstage, whom I had never seen before, singing Pinkerton. Usually the first performances are given to guys whom I know. So I wondered who this guy is, and what his claim to fame with Tony is. You have to be a fair-haired boy to get the opening night. I'd had a few, and was wondering why I didn't get this one.

Well, there's nothing I can do about that, so I settle in to check out his rendering of Pinkerton.

Tony is from the old school of opera conductors, very much the autocrat. His way is the only way. And people who don't know their parts or don't know their staging immediately get yelled at in front of the entire company. Sensitivity to performers was never a part of directing opera productions. Humiliation is the standard tool for stage directors and conductors. In his theater Tony is both.

What I immediately notice about this Pinkerton is, first of all, his splendid voice, and secondly, his amazing Italian diction. But I am very put off by his horsing around while rehearsing onstage. Offstage, OK, but not onstage. I'm baffled that Tony doesn't get all over him for that. He never takes such behavior from me or anybody else that I know. Who is this guy? Why is he so suddenly the fair-haired boy, and why does Tony pamper him like royalty?

As the rehearsal begins I quickly recognize that this tenor is a cut above the typical Amato singer. This guy has a very promising future.

I ask one of the old-timers what his name is, thinking that maybe Tony had imported somebody—a relative perhaps—from Italy.

The answer is, "Walter MacSomebody-or-other." I don't catch the last part. I assumed since his Italian is so good, he must be Italian. But when I heard the "Mac" part, I thought, That's enough. This guy's no Italian!

When I inquire further about how he knows Italian so well, the answer is that he had lived in Italy for five or six years. "He speaks it fluently," my informer went on, "which is a lot more than you can say for the rest of us."

Oh. That explains the good Italian.

But what vexes me is that his expressions and actions signal he doesn't understand a word he's singing. It belies his astonishingly good pronunciation. Why doesn't Tony correct him?

What rush of chutzpah prompts me, I'll never know. But during the first break I buttonhole "Mr. Walter," as I call him, and begin scolding him. "Mr. Walter, you have a wonderful voice and your Italian is perfect to my ear. Yet you stand up there as though you don't know what you are singing about. All I see is Walter horsing around. I wanna see Pinkerton!"

Immediately a group of colleagues gather around us as if they expect fisticuffs. Perhaps they know who he is, and perceiving I don't, they want to see what'll happen.

Walter is considerably taller than I, considerably younger, and undoubtedly stronger. He glares at me in both anger and astonishment. His eyes say to me, "Who the hell are you to tell me about performing?" At the same time, his face seems to acknowledge the truth of what I say. He replies rather lamely,

"You don't understand. It's my voice. I'm worried about my voice. I've got some important people coming to hear me, and I don't want to sing badly."

"Your voice is fine, damn it," I say heatedly. "Splendid, in fact! You've got nothing to worry about with your voice. In fact, the hell with your voice! You simply cannot stand up there on stage looking like a fool. All I see is Walter horsing around. I want to see Pinkerton."

You can cut the tension with a knife.

"But I have these people..." he protests. I cut him off:

"I don't care if Jimmy Levine himself (the Artistic Director of the Metropolitan Opera) is coming to hear you! [Yeah, sure, as if he would...] You have to sing the part. It's not about you. It's about Pinkerton. Especially if you have "important" people coming, you must sing—no, you must be the part. They'll be looking for that as much as for your voice. And your voice is fine. So get back up there and show me Pinkerton."

Stunned silence. He glares at me, and suddenly, aware of all the people standing around us, turns on his heel and heads for the bathroom.

Back onstage, he settles down and tries to be more serious about what he is doing.

Weeks after this evening and our performances, I learned that the young man was Walter MacNeil, son of Cornell MacNeil, a star baritone at the Metropolitan Opera from 1959 to 1987, singing 642 performances in twenty-six roles. Walter himself had sung in Italy and was soon to sing at City Opera. And in fact, the scuttlebutt at Amato's had it that not only did James Levine come to his Amato performance the night before mine, but Placido Domingo and Papa Cornell were there as well! Oh yeah, it was close, yet so far away!

In the meantime, a friend at Amato suggested I audition for the Regina Opera Company in Brooklyn.

Chapter 13
Regina Opera – Pagliacci

1989-1991

Up to this time my favorite roles were Rodolfo, Tamino, Alfredo, and Hoffmann, not necessarily in that order. When people asked me what my favorite role was, I'd say, "The one I'm singing right now." The one I'm singing right now was about to change: In 1989 I debuted the role of Canio in Leoncavallo's Pagliacci with Amato.

Joan thought this was my best role ever. So I wondered if anyone would hire me for it. By this time I was fifty years old, about the age I expect Canio was. While I was still good-looking enough for the younger romantic roles, I required more makeup and had to fill in my receding hair line more than I cared to admit. The top was getting rather sparse as well. "Oh well," I thought, "Canio's an older guy, so a little baldness really wouldn't matter." For Canio I could let myself be my age. This made me feel much better about the ravages of time.

Later that year I sang him in English with the Richmond Theater in Staten Island—for no fee. They called me and flattered me into helping them out of a jam because the tenor they originally counted on couldn't do it. I was always ready to help others in difficulty, so I said yes. Also, I thought it a good idea to learn the role in English. It was relatively short, so it wouldn't take long to learn it.

In May of 1991 I was hired to sing Canio for a fee by the New Rochelle Opera Company in New Rochelle, New York, a suburb just north of the city. The conductor was Gregory "Gregg" Buchalter, an assistant conductor at the Met. Artistic Director was Camille Coppola, daughter of Maestro Anton Coppola, and my friend, David Maiullo, was the rehearsal pianist for the production. David was the choir master at Wyckoff Reformed Church where Joan and I were the soloists. He became the chorus master of the New Jersey State Opera shortly after this production. In fact, it was he who got me involved with this production, and we traveled together from New Jersey to all the rehearsals and performances. The early musical rehearsals were scheduled at rehearsal rooms at the Met to accommodate Gregg's Met schedule.

Ah, now my career is gaining momentum.

Joan not only liked the way I sang it, but felt I was really convincing as Canio. Even my colleagues used to tell me that I was the only tenor who "sang" the role instead of "barked" it. Because of my age I readily identified with him, not to mention, looked the part as well.

Uh-oh! Am I getting too old for a major career?

In the fall I sang Canio with the Regina Opera Company in Brooklyn. My audition for them in some ways outshined the production itself. By this time, our son Rob attended Bergenfield High School. We lived about a half mile from the school, and Mr. Benard, his music teacher, had become a trusted mentor and friend to Rob. One day Rob came home from school and announced, "Hey Dad! Did you know that Mr. Benard is an opera fan?"

"How would I know that?"

Rob expounded on how much Mr. Benard loved opera, and concluded, "You need to meet him."

"I'd love to."

So Rob arranged a meeting at which Mr. Benard and I became instant friends, eager to swap opera yarns. In addition to being an excellent teacher, he was also a very fine pianist.

"Oh, really?" My brain started churning. Since I had already sung Canio with Amato, I felt confident about the upcoming Regina audition. But I hoped to find my own accompanist rather than rely on the usual audition pianist provided by the company. No chance to rehearse and work out the necessary details.

One Saturday afternoon Mr. Benard and I were sitting in his living room, only a few blocks away, listening to a Met broadcast of Pagliacci on the radio. When I mentioned the audition and how I would prefer to have my own accompanist rather than take my chances with the company one, Mr. Benard offered his services.

Since I didn't know if he could play a difficult opera score, I instantly dashed home to retrieve a score of Pagliacci so I could audition him. I was amazed and impressed with his sight-reading. He followed me instinctively and felt each nuance of the music. Truly, he was a gifted accompanist. Opera scores can be devilish to play on the piano because they are orchestral reductions of all the instruments, often requiring skills above and beyond ordinary piano literature.

Over the course of the next few weeks we worked on the two major arias, "Vesti la giubba" and "No! Pagliaccio non son!" The latter presents fiendish challenges for the accompanist, but Mr. Benard tackled them extremely well. He explained with a modest smile that although he had never played this music, he had the sound of it in his soul from listening to this opera so much.

On the appointed day, I drove him to the audition in Brooklyn, which took place on the Regina's performing stage. Gathered before me were quite a few people, none of whom I knew. I wondered to myself who they all might be and why there were so many there to hear the auditions. Even at the Bronx Opera I didn't recall so many people.

After singing "Vesti la giubba," there was applause and smiles of approbation all around. Relaxing a bit, I looked out at the gathered assembly and suddenly noticed for the first time Alejandro "Alex" Guzman, whom I knew from the Bronx Opera, where he had been the chorus master. He was now a principal conductor with the Regina Opera. He smiled broadly and applauded enthusiastically along with everyone else after I sang.

I beamed at him and stepped over to the edge of the stage. "Alex, what are you doing here?" I called.

Getting up, he sauntered over to greet me and replied, "When I heard you were coming I just had to be here to hear you!"

It was difficult to describe my feelings about this moment. The knee-jerk reaction in my head was I wondered why he wanted to hear me, and is he being sarcastic? After all the frustration and abuse I'd grown accustomed to, to have an opera conductor tell me how eager he was to hear me hardly rang a positive bell in my jaded head. But the positive ring in his voice and smile on his face beamed the truth. When his enthusiasm finally hit me, I had to stop myself from choking up from feeling so richly blessed.

I reached down from the stage and shook his hand heartily and introduced him to Mr. Benard. I then looked at the other directors, to whom I had been introduced in the meantime, and offered to sing, "Pagliacci, non son . . .since we went to all the trouble to prepare it for you!" indicating Mr. Benard now standing beside me.

Everyone laughed and responded by clapping and exclaiming, "Yes! Yes, please do!"

Mr. Benard and I acquitted ourselves so well that when we finished the entire group jumped to their feet and gave us a standing ovation. It felt like Sherrill Milnes' debut at City Opera, but this time it was me they were applauding.

The directors hired me right on the spot, as they had done at my Susannah audition with the Bronx Opera several years before.

I thank Mr. Benard's masterful support for that success. I could not have been more pleased. Beaming smiles and vigorous handshakes again!

And—all this and he wouldn't take a penny for his services.

You see, Dad? There's more to it than the money. They made me feel like a celebrity. Recognition and being the best you can be. Isn't that what you always preached at me?

Of course, I latched on to Mr. Benard as an accompanist for future endeavors. We began to make plans to prepare material for concerts as well as working on opera roles. He was as pleased as I was with our new partnership.

Tragically, only a month or two later, Mr. Benard died suddenly of a rare, inherited disease. He was only in his thirties. What a shock and loss to us all! The funeral parlor was so packed that I waited well over an hour to get inside the front door, a fitting tribute to him. He was a much-beloved teacher, friend, and colleague, not just to all of his students and me, but also to the entire Bergenfield community. I was bereft to lose such a friend and newly found co-artist.

As we were about to leave the Regina hall, Alex button-holed me again to tell me that he wanted me to sing Pollione in his upcoming production of Bellini's Norma, which was scheduled for June. I couldn't believe my ears and tried to act as if this sort of thing happened all the time.

There were two casts for Pagliacci. My cast included my baritone friend, Eugene Green as Tonio, whom I had met during Magic Flute with the Bronx Opera some years before. Gene lived in Tenafly, only two or three miles from our house in Bergenfield. Since he had invited me to sing at the synagogue where he was the cantor, also in Brooklyn, he and I commuted together to rehearsals for both synagogue and opera whenever we could. On the drive back and forth we discussed the staging and worked out details of how we would do things onstage.

Gene had sung with many regional companies across the country, and he was a great mentor. He had also taught me the ins and outs of stage makeup during the Bronx Magic Flute production. By day Gene was a set designer and artist for ABC TV. Both Gene and his wife Ethel were professional artists, so he came to the art of makeup with a unique background and talent.

I would drive to his house in Tenafly and he would drive the two of us into Brooklyn. On the way, when we weren't talking shop, he regaled me with jokes and stories until my sides split, usually about other singers.

Gene also schlepped me into Manhattan a couple of times to his voice lessons with his teacher, noted baritone Dan Merriman, who had become one of the important voice teachers in New York. I already knew Dan because he had substituted numerous times at Hebrew Tabernacle. He also managed his and his wife's busy singing careers. Gene wanted me to study with Dan, thinking he could help me with my breath problems. Since I was still working with Linda Hall and Giovanni, I didn't feel right about switching.

As a result of this Pagliacci production, conductor Gregory Ortega asked me to sing Dick Johnson in Puccini's La Fanciulla del West. He told me, "I love this opera. It's one of the most underrated operas in the repertory. Johnson is a perfect role for you."

Later I mentioned this to Fran Garber, Regina's producer, who said, "Yes I know – Greg has mentioned this to me several times. But the cast requirements for Fanciulla are too much for us. Where would we get that many principal singers?"

Greg, determined to at least do a scene from this opera, arranged for me to sing the Act 1 duet at one of Regina's regularly scheduled concert series with none other than Met soprano Lynn Owen, whom he knew personally. She had sung Minnie many times in her distinguished career.

After our first rehearsal together she invited me to her upper West Side apartment to work on the scene. She had worked out some simple staging. When I arrived, she and her husband, Richard, greeted me like royalty. She had prepared a table with goodies and coffee, and immediately invited me to sit down to "get to know each other a bit." I felt not only welcome, but she treated me like a colleague as well. What a class act she was.

When we finally got down to the business of singing, she coached me in my part, and showed me the staging she'd thought of. This was great for me because I don't like standing still on stage. Movement not only helps you relax, but it helps to tell the story, be it opera or concert.

We were quite a hit with the opera-savvy Brooklyn audience. That was the only time in my career that I sang with a Met diva. I felt as though I had arrived. It felt so-o-o good!

Hey Dad – I sang with a Metropolitan Opera soprano! Am I on my way or what?

Somehow it didn't feel right to ask her to help me with my career. Could she have? I didn't want to embarrass her in case she couldn't.

Rehearsals for Pagliacci went smoothly enough, resulting in a performance of which J. Sambra Shiepe of the Brooklyn Spectator on April 3, 1991 wrote:

> The Regina Opera Company presented Leoncavallo's I Pagliacci recently, as part of the company's 20th year celebration.
>
> The fine assembly of participants resulted in a splendid production, keeping pace with the lofty standards of Brooklyn's premiere regional opera company, which its devoted audiences have learned to respect.
>
> When this reviewer was present, making his debut was tenor Robert Mitchell, cast in the title role. He gave a thrilling rendition of the great tenor aria, 'Vesti la giubba,' registering the heart-rending agony of every brooding emotion dramatically, winning the admiration of the enthusiastic audience.
> (Used by permission)

Regina Opera - Norma

Bellini's Norma was never in what most people would regard as the "standard repertoire," and I have to say: one, I didn't know it, and two, I never thought I would sing it. When Alex first asked me to sing it, I hesitated because I did not know the opera. I didn't even have a score of it. It wasn't until after the Pagliacci production was over that I bought a score and began studying it. I called Alex and told him Pollione was "tuu drah-MAH-tik" for me.

Mme Ryss would have been proud of me.

Immediately Alex objected. "Look, Bob, you sounded great as Canio. How dramatic can you get? Besides, I like the way you sing Canio. You sing it, not bark it. That's what I need for Pollione. How about it?"

"Much of it lies too low for me," I said, shaking my head over the phone.

"That's what I thought you'd say," he countered. "I have terrific news for you. I came across Mario's [not Lanza] changes to Bellini's score and I am dying to use them. They're much higher than the original. B-flats and high As all over the place. Perfect for your voice. There are not many tenors who could manage this—but you can." (Mario was one of the great singers of the nineteenth century, creating roles as diverse as Pollione and numerous Verdi heroes. He also distinguished himself as Don Giovanni, a baritone part.)

How could I turn down such exuberant affirmation? Haven't I been looking for this very thing all my life?

Norma is one of those operas in and out of favor, not because of the opera, but because it requires extraordinary singers in every voice category, unlike most operas that tend to feature one or two voices. In Norma, the soprano and mezzo parts both require long ranges and technical razzmatazz. The opera requires a leading tenor and bass as well.

I was fortunate to have soprano Phyliss Falletta as Norma. She not only carried the part admirably, but knew the opera so well that she coached me in my part. As an accomplished pianist, and fluent in Italian as well, she was a God-send to me. The Italian text of Norma is more like Shakespeare than the conversational language of Boheme or Traviata. It was hard enough for me to learn those operas, but this one brought great challenges. Phyliss spent many hours in her lovely Bay Ridge apartment in Brooklyn drilling Pollione into my head.

Alex's great research benefitted both of us. We spent many hours working the score together.

The reviews told the final story. After giving Phyllis well-deserved praise, Nino Pantano of the Brooklyn Graphic Weekly said of me of our June 1 premiere:

Norma's Roman warrior lover, Pollione, was heroically sung by tenor Robert Mitchell. Indeed, his act one aria, "Meco all'altar di Venere" was a tour de force. His is a solid voice, dramatic, but also able to sing sweetly when called upon to do so. When confronted by Norma, who secretly loved him and has borne him two children, and by his new love, Adalgisa, he looked like a boy with his hand caught in a cookie jar (or two cookie jars in this instance). However, his humble demeanor quickly changes when he tries to force Adalgisa to go with him. Norma is furious with Pollione but forbearing to the innocent Adalgisa.

(Used by permission)

But I almost didn't sing this opera. When we began the staging rehearsals I was not at all pleased with our stage director's method of conducting rehearsals. She would start every rehearsal at the beginning of the opera and run through it from beginning to end, or as far as the evening would take us, which usually was not very far. My early concern was whether we'd ever get to Acts 3 and 4 of the opera.

Moreover, throughout Norma there are large chorus scenes, sometimes interspersed with ensemble or solo scenes. It was maddening to sit through hours of chorus for five minutes of a principal scene, and then go sit down again. After working all day at Scholastic, I had to drive from New Jersey to Brooklyn, a fifty-mile round trip through Manhattan—with numerous tolls, by the way. I soon began to strongly resent sitting around, sometimes for an hour or more, while the director rehearsed the chorus or other cast members. Everyone started to gripe.

Several times I tried to persuade the director to organize the rehearsals so that people's time would not be so wasted. But she was obstinate. "I couldn't do that. Too much work. Too many people involved." And she would walk away from me.

One evening I got so frustrated with her that I shouted, "Look, you're wasting my time! I'm sorry you're too damned lazy to set up a proper schedule for rehearsals. I've never worked this way in the past, and I'm not going to work this way now. I come all the way from New Jersey, it's one hell of a trip, and I'm not being paid as you are, nor am I reimbursed for my travel, so I'll be damned if I'm going to sit around here doing nothing. [Oh, Lord! I sounded just like Jack!] And I'm not speaking just for myself—everyone is inconvenienced by your incompetency. Either you do as I suggest, or you can find yourself another tenor."

And I turned on my heel and walked out, shouting all the way that I simply refuse to waste my time like this. "It's just not worth it to schlep all the way to Brooklyn to sit around here doing nothing!"

Fran Garber, who was not only Regina's Producer, but a principal of the company, and was singing the role of Clotilde, immerged out of the crowd during my little scena, taking it all in. I hadn't noticed her. When I started to leave, she immediately came running after me. I don't think she expected me to walk off the set like that. She caught up and grabbed me by the arm, begging me to stay. "Bob, please! You can't walk out like this."

"Oh, no? Just watch me." And I tried to pull away.

But she held on all the tighter and assured me that I was right and that, as producer of the Regina Opera Company, she would address this situation immediately.

"Immediately?" I couldn't imagine her taking precious rehearsal time for a meeting. I looked her sternly in the eye, then saw her resolve, and, not sure if she could handle this situation, slowly nodded my head.

She marched back into the rehearsal hall and louder than I ever heard her, called all the directors and staff of the company into a closed-door meeting right then and there. They followed her like sheep to the slaughter.

The cast rushed over to me, gathered around and thanked me both for standing up to the errant director, and for not abandoning the show. We all waited nervously, not sure whether I, or the director would go. Usually a director wins out over one singer in these small companies, singers being easier to replace than directors. They had another tenor who'd be glad to sing all the performances, thought I. I did it many times myself.

But of course, it wasn't just about me. In any case, if they did not change the rehearsal proceedings, I was still determined to leave.

When they emerged, Fran assembled the cast and assured us that rehearsals from now on would be arranged as efficiently as possible. I felt vindicated, and quite glad of the company's direction. Fran recognized this crisis was not about me, but affected all of us, including chorus members who had to sit around when we principals were rehearsing our scenes. And so I gladly—and proudly—stayed on.

As I wrote this story, I tracked down Alex on the Internet, and he verified my recollection of the events as I have described them. He added that they never hired that person again.

There is yet another nail-biting story connected with this production. As show people know, for reasons of backup most companies double cast their principal roles. Even celebrities in big-time productions have covers.

Performances had long since been announced for Saturday, June 1, Sunday afternoon on June 2, and the following weekend on June 8 and 9. I was scheduled to sing June 1, and again on June 9.

Joan's brother, Fred, after a long, protracted battle with pancreatic cancer, succumbed to it a day or so before the opening of Norma. While his death was expected, it nevertheless was a great blow to us. Fred was only sixty-four and much beloved by family and friends alike. In my grief, I totally disconnected from Norma, so it never occurred to me to mention to anyone at Regina that a viewing was scheduled on the afternoon of June 2.

There is an unwritten code—well, unwritten for companies without contracts—that members of each cast are considered standbys for their counterparts for all performances in which they are not scheduled. Regina did not have contracts with us singers. In a fleeting thought, I convinced myself that we would be back from the viewing in time to cover my counterpart because that performance wasn't until 4:00, so I never gave it another thought. Also, I had no idea he had the flu all week, or I would have planned a bit differently.

So we went to the viewing without a concern in the world. When we left the funeral parlor it was around 4:00, and Norma was the farthest thing from my mind. The family invited us to a supper after which we were to come back for the evening viewing. We decided to go home in between to feed the dog and to rest a bit before the next viewing at 7:00. The funeral home was about a half hour away from Bergenfield.

So it was about 4:30 when we walked in the door. Joan noticed the phone was blinking. She pushed the Play button and a woman's voice neither of us recognized was furiously shouting something about somebody named Norma, and said that I was to "get over there instantly."

Puzzled, I said to Joan, "I don't know anyone named Norma."

"Oh my goodness, Bob, it's the opera! They need you to sing."

"To sing? I'm not supposed to sing today. They know that. What's going on?"

"Didn't you hear the message?"

"I couldn't make it out. Look, I'm tired. I want to lay down."

"Michael is sick. He's already gone on because they couldn't reach you, but he'll never make it to the end. You've got to get to Brooklyn!"

"To Brooklyn? On a day like this? The weather's gorgeous. The roads'll be so packed I'll never get there before the opera ends! Forget about it!"

"Stop yammering and get in the car and get moving! Now!"

Normally I applied my own makeup at home, much to the amusement of toll collectors—no E-Z Pass in those days. I always allowed plenty of time to get to the theater. But here I was, dressed in my best suit and tie, which I never wore to the theater. Joan virtually pushed me out the door. I jumped in the car and started to drive.

Now—which way to get to Brooklyn? Usually I drove through Manhattan, but this Saturday was a perfect outing day. I imagined the city would be clogged to a standstill. Also, no traffic radio on a Sunday, so I decided not to chance Manhattan, but to take the New Jersey Turnpike to Staten Island and into Brooklyn via the Verrazano Bridge.

It's a bit longer, but should be quicker...

As I drove south on the Turnpike my vision of quicker became a nightmare. Near Newark Airport, traffic congealed into a parking lot. My anxiety level went off the charts. Then I saw the cause: an accident on the Goethals Bridge backing up traffic on to the turnpike.

"Yikes!" I screamed. "Now what do I do?"

In desperation I decided to take the Outer Bridge Crossing and come back across Staten Island.   It's only a few miles from here.

I moved to the left tarmac and screeched past stopped cars on the highway. As soon as I passed the Goethals exit the traffic thinned out. I drove. Then I drove faster. And faster.

Where in the world is this exit? I thought it was a few miles.

Twenty-five miles and as many minutes later, I saw the signs to it. I paid my toll and scrambled back to the north side of Staten Island, another twenty minutes. When I finally got to the Verrazano Bridge I rushed across it.

Now where do I go? I was lost. Oh my Lord, I never come this way. How can I find the Regina Cieli Church? It's Twelfth Avenue and Sixty-

Fifth Street, right? Or is it Twelfth Street and Sixty-Fifth Avenue? Oh Lord!

No cell phones...

Well, somehow the Good Lord got me there. Finding the church is a total blank in my memory, but I remember Fran frantically waiting for me at the door. As it happened, it was between acts three and four. Without a word passing between us, I undressed and struggled with my costume, she helping as she could, and when not needed, she dabbed some makeup on my face and lips. "Never mind the eyes," were the only words spoken. In my state of mind I didn't know which end was up, anyway.

I must have survived, because Jennie Schulman of Back Stage said:

> *As Pollione, the alternate tenor, Robert Mitchell, stepped in for the final act to show us how tremendously effective the role can be, both vocally and histrionically.*
> (Used by permission)

While this was a welcome tribute to my performance, I have always felt bad for Michael, the alternate Polline. He was sick, yet bravely got onstage and carried the part for three acts, a tribute to his artistic and musical integrity. The next weekend he got a great review by Ms. Shiepe of the Brooklyn Spectator.

Hey Dad! What do you think of me now? Still think I'm a tinker's damn?

Somebody's bound to notice me...

Chapter 14
A Big Name Voice Teacher

1987 – 1989

In the wake of the Opera Classics Butterfly, my sickness, and the falling out with Giovanni, Linda decided to send me to another teacher. She wanted to move me up to the big time, to work with a major teacher in the opera world. She knew that this would stress our budget, but she felt I needed this kind of exposure. It would help me grow as an artist and also put me on the radar screen of regional and major houses. Budget-wise the cost for lessons tripled. Experience-wise, well, here's what happened:

The teacher she had in mind had been a mainstay baritone at City Opera for at least twenty years, she told me. His name was Richard Fredericks. He also sang at the Met and appeared from time to time on TV. She recommended him highly as he was not only a good teacher, but had students singing in regional and major houses. She also believed that he would champion my career as no one had before. So I went to him with great expectations.

When I first began my studies with Dick in the spring of 1988, he was living on Seventy-First Street east of Broadway. He was married to a vivacious young blonde with whom he had fathered an adorable blond baby boy, about two at the time. When I showed up for my lessons this playful toddler was also on hand to entertain and be entertained. We had lots of fun together, and he usually had to be distracted away from me to begin my lesson. Typically it was his lovely mother who came to the rescue.

In many ways Dick was the best teacher I ever had. In the first lesson he explained exactly what he was going to teach me. He illustrated his technique as follows:

"Suppose you spot your friend Gloria across Forty-Second Street, and you need to speak to her right away. You wouldn't say 'Gloria!' in this conversational voice, would you?"

I shook my head.

"No! You would say it like this: GLO-O-O-O-RIA!" And out came a baritone high F that shook the room and rattled the windows.

His point needed no further argument. I shared with him Mme Ryss' notion of "singing is speech," an idea that resonated with him. He based his technique, he told me, largely upon his educational background as an engineer. "Pop the belly and rest!" was how a singer should breathe. He explained that by popping the belly, a partial vacuum would be created inside the body and the air would flow in by itself with no assistance needed by the singer other than to relax the throat and let the air pass freely. The singer's job was to stay out of the way and let nature do the rest.

It made scientific sense, I confess, but as the weeks wore on I could not get the hang of it. It didn't feel natural to me. I did not argue with him, but kept trying to get it right. Nevertheless, he persistently stopped me for "pulling off the breath," his words. Many times he got in my face (quite literally) about it.

Again, the breath! Is it I? What's the matter with me? Why can't I get a good breath for singing? Why can't I sustain the line as other singers do?

As my lessons progressed I often thought of Franco Corelli's circus act of holding the high-A in Turandot, and wept. I thought of Jussi Björling's and Nicolai Gedda's endless breath-lines, and groaned. Dick himself had an incredible breath line which he proudly displayed for me as an example on every occasion the subject came up. He could also sing all my tenor notes, by the way, which was a bit embarrassing for me—don't ask me why.

OK, so he could hold them longer than I could, but the sound was nothing you'd want to listen to. But why couldn't anyone teach me how to manage my breath properly?

Dick's ideas about breath support and voice placement—which he called "singing in the honker" was essentially the same as Giovanni's, and they helped me a great deal. His concrete images made the concept come alive for me.

While Mme Ryss and Mr. Singher had taught me to keep the breath away from the singing mechanism, Dick insisted that that was precisely my problem: that I pulled my breath off the support. His notion worked for me, and my singing improved.

But my shortness of breath remained. I used to tell people I could sing all the high notes that Pavarotti could—including a high D—I just couldn't hold them as long.

Nevertheless, Dick was enthusiastic about my progress, and began to tell me that I was a world-class singer. The beauty of my voice, my musicality, and sensitivity to music and drama placed me with the best singers in the world, he said. The only reason I could not get singing jobs was my self-image: that I thought of myself as too old, too fat, and I believed that life had passed me by. He told me to lose weight and get a toupee to look younger. "You might even wear makeup to important auditions," he suggested, "…to look younger."

I never did conquer the weight problem entirely, despite many efforts. My experience had been that every time I lost weight, my voice got lighter, something I didn't like. Joan and I had lost weight on Weight Watchers' plan and later on the Columbia diet system. In both cases I had lost about thirty or forty pounds. I felt good health-wise with less weight, and I looked good and could breathe easier; but my voice always seemed paler and weaker to me. It helped somewhat with the breathing, but I still could not hold a high note as long as the big boys.

Thus I was conflicted, so my weight became a catch-22. I always wondered how Pavarotti sang so well carrying all that weight around. And then there was Domingo. I remember at one point in his career he lost a lot of weight—as did Callas in hers. I could hear the loss of tone and power in both their voices as a result.

I did get a toupee, however, which Joan thought totally ridiculous. She always laughed or guffawed when I wore it. I have never understood quite why. But I'll never forget the look on people's faces the day I wore it to work at Scholastic—you'd think I was wearing a dress or something. Some diverted their eyes. Still others had to repress a giggle or two. Some actually said they liked it—made me look younger—which after all, was the point.

I never wore it to work again, and resolved to use it only for the stage, which I did.

When I asked Dick about helping me build a career, he cussed and said that he wished he could, but that he was on the outs with all the important people. He claimed he was being slighted by everyone, mentioning some prominent names, and that it was no fault of his, and so on. Nevertheless, he encouraged me by citing several important singers whose careers began late in their lives.

Dick had an upbeat, positive way of saying things, much like a charismatic huckster. I believed he believed in me, so I hung in there with him and continued to perform operas and concerts. Both Dick and Linda helped me find auditions and other opportunities.

Then one day after about a year with him, I had a lesson that ended all lessons. I really couldn't say exactly how it happened, not so much that I want to keep it private, even though I was trying to be discreet about it, but because it was so traumatic that I honestly don't remember precisely what happened. I have no doubt that my subconscious has simply blotted much of it out.

I made a critical comment about his support of me, probably to the effect that I wondered if he was taking my money and had no intention of helping me with a career. Come to think of it, though he sent me to people, he never recommended me to anyone, nor had he referred me, nor introduced me to any company. As I said already, whenever the subject came up, he always went into his, "I'm on the outs with everyone I can't help you" routine.

But this time I said something that he took very personally. Whatever it was, he flew into a rage that should have earned him an Oscar. As he was adept at it, he got in my face, I could feel his spit on my face, shouting obscenities, and subjected me to the worst verbal abuse I have ever experienced in my life.

"You son of a bitch, you [the names he actually called me were far too obscene for this book], I'm the one who stood up for you! I encouraged you! I've taught you how to sing and told you how to change your life, and how to become a star! And what do you do? ..." On and on it went. It could have been twenty seconds or twenty minutes for all I can remember.

He made my father seem like a kitten. My feet were nailed to the floor, my arms strapped to my sides. I wanted to punch him in the mouth, but no part of me could move. Dick was nearly a head taller than I, and in pretty good shape. In fact, he looked like and was built a lot like Sean Connery. I was petrified, nailed to the spot, unable to move or breathe. It was a nightmare that wouldn't go away. I was really scared.

As suddenly as he started yelling, he stopped—I don't know why. After a while I had tuned him out, so I was stunned when he stopped yelling. I no longer felt his breath, but the spit was still there.

Perhaps he realized how excessive he was, perhaps he saw the utter despair and fear in my face and decided it was no use, or perhaps, well, who knows what he was thinking? We never discussed it. It makes no difference in any case. What happened, happened.

Feeling like an out-of-body robot, I turned to the piano, picked up my music and the rest of my belongings from the nearby chair, and walked solemnly to the door. He was standing in the middle of the room, so I had to navigate around him to get to the door. Without looking at him or saying a word, I walked slowly but determinedly, opened the door, and walked out. Neither of us spoke, nor did he try to stop me. I believe he just stood where he was. I don't know, nor do I care.

For me it was the most frightful experience in my life, and I dare say, the most unique. I still don't know quite what to make of it. Looking back on it, I suppose God had a reason for it, but he hasn't clued me in.

I never saw Dick again.

He called me the following Monday to try to convince me to come back, and that I still had a shot at a career. I expected the call and had prepared to lambast him for his unprofessional conduct, and demand an apology, but when I got on the phone, some powerful inner voice took me elsewhere. Instead of confronting him, I blamed myself. Maybe it was cowardice, or maybe it was the prompting of the Holy Spirit, I don't know.

I told him I could no longer spend the lesson money on myself. At my age, nearly fifty, my dream had become a fool's errand (just as Dad had said, though I did not say that to Dick). If I couldn't get on a stage with the big boys, then a major career was never going to happen at my age. It was time to chuck it in. I owed my family some attention instead of pursuing my own goals.

I told him I was not coming back. He argued, I let him. In my mind I revisited his motives for teaching me at ninety dollars an hour. I knew he had lost a couple of students and things were not going well for him financially—he told me that himself. He needed the money. Was that his motive? I can't get in his head to assess his motives, but trust was on the ropes. As he babbled on I very quietly returned the phone to its hook.

Something in me had snapped; I just couldn't go on pursuing this dream anymore. I had some serious thinking to do.

Did Dad have his victory after all? Was it all just a pipe dream?

The fact remains that Dick moved me to whole new level of singing, for which I am eternally grateful, and I will always have the delight of his declaring me a world-class singer.

You can check out my singing here (turn up the volume):
Bob Mitchell sings on YouTube
http://www.youtube.com/watch?v=Cu_FwjqK44M&playnext=1&list=PL6E5A80279FF14DB5&feature=results_main

Chapter 15
How Do We Go On From Here

1988 – 1991

Joan and I discussed what happened at great length. Our sons were both adolescents by this time, and I lamented how much of their growing up I had missed. Rob was taking violin lessons and he was so talented we wanted to buy him a really fine instrument, which began at $3,000. Little by little we were also discovering that he had special needs in school. He hated math and rebelled against it. His gifts for language, reading, and writing were already in the fore. He was composing music and writing plays, but couldn't seem to complete any task he undertook. His room was littered with manuscripts and drawings; I wondered how he knew what he was working on. His room, as you might imagine, had long since been a source of contention.

His teachers complained that he didn't pay attention in class and that he was difficult to keep on task. We knew Rob is intelligent and gifted, so why was he having all this trouble in school? Well, first of all, we needed to pay more attention to him, I needed to spend more time with him, so we began to work with him at home, and began family counseling as well. We also enrolled him in special after-school classes to help him keep up. All of which costs big bucks.

By the way, all these issues with Rob had been building up for some time, so the voice lesson experience was simply the eye-opener for both Joan and me. Later Rob was diagnosed with A.D.D.

While Randy had no such challenges, he wanted to take guitar lessons along with his violin lessons, plus he wanted to study Tae Kwon Do. All these expenses were piling up and it became crystal clear that I could not continue to spend our meager resources on my singing.

At one point back in the early eighties I had sat down and figured out that I had invested approximately $300,000 in my singing from Mannes up to that point. What I earned through singing was a tiny fraction of that. I could hear Dad laughing and saying 'I told you so.'

In the spring of 1991, I was still singing, and Tony asked me to sing Alvaro in Verdi's La Forza Del Destino, and he even asked me if I would be interested in singing Verdi's Otello. I had now come full circle from Mr. Fontana. The aria he expected me to sing as an adolescent, "Oh, tu che in seno agli angeli" now fit nicely in my voice. I had even worked on it with Dick Fredericks. I also began to study Otello on my own. Mme. Ryss had passed away in the eighties, but I could hear her strident voice yelling at me about these "dra-MAH-tik" roles, especially, Otello, one of the most "dra-MAH-tik" roles in all of opera.

On another front, Michael Spierman of the Bronx Opera had invited me to sit on his side of the desk to listen to auditions. I had recently sung Sam in their production of Susannah, and later sang a small role in their production of Vaughan Williams' Sir John in Love. Michael wanted me to experience what directors listen and look for in singers. I had offered to help backstage and even coach other singers as needed in productions in which I did not sing.

Listening to those auditions was an eye-opener for me. As we discussed each candidate, I came to realize how important appearance is and how much less important voice is, contrary to what I had always believed. For example, we listened to a tenor with whom I had sung in a previous production, a singer I favored over the one the directors wanted. My reasons were vocal. They agreed my man was a better singer, but said he was too short for the soprano they had chosen. The tenor they wanted was okay vocally, but he was taller and quite handsome—he really "looked" the part and sang it satisfactorily. When I saw the soprano with him I immediately agreed they made a handsome couple.

In my life as a singer I would have felt it unfair that the best voice did not get the part, but sitting on the other side of the table, it was a very different perspective.

I had taken another step in the world of opera. A step up.

Several other opera companies made overtures to me to sing various roles. How exciting for me! But I had to say no to all of them because Joan and I made a life-changing decision.

Joan was not happy with her life as a secretary; she wanted something better. A friend suggested that she look into becoming a counselor or therapist. When she did, she found it quite daunting in terms of money, time, and qualifications. At some point she mentioned her predicament to our pastor at the time, the Reverend Doctor Willis Jones at the Wyckoff

Reformed Church in Wyckoff, New Jersey, where we were the paid soloists.

Willis suggested seminary.

"Seminary?" Joan asked. "Why seminary?"

"Well," Willis explained, "as part of preparing for the ministry you'll receive training in counseling. Maybe you could find a career path that way."

The idea intrigued her, so she applied to the Reformed Church seminary in New Brunswick, New Jersey. The New Brunswick Theological Seminary is the eastern seminary for the Reformed Church in America, the denomination in which we were currently soloists, but also, we had joined the Wyckoff Reformed Church and had become very active in it above and beyond singing. We made many life-long friends there as well.

In July of 1991, Joan took her first courses leading toward a Master of Divinity degree. In August, she and I were sitting in the living room talking about her experience at NBTS. She was excited about studying again. She loved her teachers and her advisor. I said something to the effect that she would become so damned smart I wouldn't be able to talk to her anymore. She replied, "Why don't you come, too?"

"Sure, why not? Then I could study Hebrew as I always wanted to," I said rather flippantly. As I was to learn later in my seminary experience, studying Hebrew was not the right reason to attend seminary, but it seemed a good idea at the time.

So, in September, 1991, Joan and I began seminary together.

In the meantime I was rehearsing for the upcoming Carmen in November. Since I had a number of scenes with the fiery protagonist, she and I decided we needed more time to work out our staging together. I was still singing at the Hebrew Tabernacle, and prevailed upon them to let us use the downstairs social hall as a rehearsal stage. Debra Kitabjian, my superb-in-every-respect Carmen, met me there several times, and we also sang several concerts together in downtown Manhattan.

Despite beginning seminary, I had no plans for retiring from opera. As I mentioned, Tony had roles in mind for me, and despite the teacher set-back and my career despair at that time, my opera career seemed to be taking off again. In addition, other opera companies approached me about roles. My career seemed to be on track. Pumped up, I felt I could handle singing, seminary, and work.

The night of November 9, Debbie and I sang our only Carmen performance together. With a number of highly emotionally charged scenes we had carefully worked out, we both threw ourselves into them, no holds barred. I played José as a naïve kid gradually descending into a morose, violence-laden madness from the moment she began to make fun of me when I visited her after prison. By the end of the opera my whole emotional being was like a time bomb waiting to explode. The last straw was when she threw back the ring I had given her. I (José) stabbed her to death on the spot.

Our portrayals were so successful that we received a standing ovation, rare at the Amato Theater. Drenched in sweat, spent emotionally, we joined hands to receive it together.

Afterward I felt on top of the world. I had achieved what I set out to achieve: recognition for my art. Did I achieve my goal of singing like Mario? Oh, yes I did indeed, but even better, I was now a much more refined and polished singer than Mario ever was. To be sure, Lanza had his own charisma and vocal excitement, but I achieved something more precious than his raw passion. The more I learned about singing and opera, the more I aspired to the brilliant sound of Pavarotti, the vocal and artistic mastery of Domingo, the lyrical power of Jussi Björling, and the literary elegance of Nicolai Gedda.

If Dad equated success with fame and fortune, then in that he won. Instead, I achieved something far more precious: a high level of artistry, vocally, musically and dramatically, that far surpassed anything Lanza could claim.

From here on I looked forward to working on the new roles Tony and others had invited me to do.

However, that performance on that moonlit November evening turned out to be my swan song in opera. After that Carmen performance, the following Monday Joan and I had to drive the fifty miles to seminary after work. I was still exhausted from that performance and I asked her, "Would you please drive?" She was never eager to, but she understood how wiped out I was and agreed without a fuss.

I almost fell asleep in class. I snored on the way home late that night—classes ended around 11:00 p.m., and the drive home generally took us, assuming no traffic problems, almost two hours. On the way home we would stop at the Meadowlands to pick up Joan's car, and then drive both cars home. I followed her so as to keep awake. The following morning I had to get up with the birds to catch the bus to work.

That morning my feet were in slow motion and I almost missed the last bus from Bergenfield. From the New York station the rush to the subway seemed endless. I slipped and fell down the subway steps. I arrived at Scholastic soaking wet from sweat, trousers ripped, skinned knee, bleeding, and feeling a downer that spoke volumes to me.

At last it became abundantly clear that I could no longer sing opera productions and meet the heavy demands of seminary study and the fatiguing travel back and forth to seminary and manage my career at Scholastic, which had reached twenty-four years by this time. The choice was agonizing, but inevitable. I had known it, but literally had to stumble to be convinced to say goodbye.

Still, I look back on my singing career with a glowing and thankful heart. Setbacks, mistakes and disappointments all go with the territory— it's called life. But I certainly miss being onstage singing my heart out.

Few people have had the opportunity to do what I did for as long as I did. It was a joy, and I look back with a mixture of pride, love, as well as a hard pinch of regret for all the things I did wrong. On the other hand, I had what few people had: three diverse, successful careers: as a business manager at Scholastic, as a pastor, and yes, as a singer. In addition, we had a family that stayed together.

Moreover, as I reflect on what I achieved, I am struck by my guess that even singers like Mario Lanza, or Domingo (who sang 140 roles in a slew of languages), or Björling, or any other singer you might name, did not experience all I did. Oh yes, they had fame and fortune, but did they:

•Sing small parts such as the Priest in Magic Flute and Tinca in Il Tabbarro.

•Sing early Renaissance music in Harold Brown's Renaissance Chorus of New York.

•Sing as chorister under Maestro Alfredo Silipigni (New Jersey State Opera), Maestro Robert Lawrence (Friends of French Opera, Carnegie Hall), with Dave Brubeck (La Fiesta de la Posada) at First Presbyterian Church in Ridgewood, New Jersey, under Rob Davis.

•Sing as section leader and soloist in church choirs from Baptist and Assembly of God across the religious spectrum to Roman Catholic (in Latin) and Greek Orthodox (in Greek), including Presbyterian churches in

Englewood, Ridgewood, (NJ), Scarsdale, NYC and Queens, Episcopalian churches in Englewood, Paterson, Long Island, and New York City for over forty years.

•Sing in Reform and Conservative synagogues in NY and NJ for thirty years.

•Enjoy a thirty-year career in a large publishing firm.

•Go on to become a pastor, or

•Sing these roles: Cadi in Barber of Bagdad, Sam in Susannah, Dick Warrington in Naughty Marietta, Camille in Merry Widow, Kaspar in Amahl and the Night Visitors, both Belmonte and Pedrillo in Abduction from the Seraglio, Tsar Berendey in Snow Maiden (Rimsky-Korsakov), Caius in Sir John in Love (Vaughan-Williams), Rev. Parris in Crucible (Ward), Joseph in Joseph and the Amazing Technicolor Dreamcoat, and last, but by no means least, according to David Schechter, I am the only tenor in history to have sung full productions of Verdi's first and last operas: Riccardo in Oberto and Fenton in Falstaff?

Yes, I did all that without a tip of the hat from anyone. Unheralded as it was, my singing career was rich and fruitful, and I thank God for the blessings it brought me. Moreover, as I write these lines, Joan and I recently celebrated our fiftieth wedding anniversary.

How many stars achieved all that?

We have two lovely granddaughters and a precious new grandson… Thanks be to God!

Epilogue
Aftermath

1994

Part of our seminary training included two courses in preaching. The great thing about completing them successfully in the Reformed Church in America (RCA) is that you are awarded a license to preach while still a seminarian. The RCA does not permit just anyone to stand up and preach. You have to be licensed or ordained. (RCA ordains Preaching Elders as lay preachers.) For us that meant that we could preach for other pastors on vacation or away from their pulpits for whatever reason. New Brunswick Theological Seminary encouraged its students to take advantage of its referral system, especially in the summer. Joan and I found that we were busy for most of the summers in our last couple of years in seminary.

My first pulpit was unforgettable for a number of reasons. The only reason that concerns this memoir is that I found myself getting hoarse half way through the service. Having to do the opening prayers, announcements, and liturgy, by the time I got to the sermon I was hoarse for much of it, not to mention the following pastoral prayers—very embarrassing. Thank heaven for the microphone.

This experience shocked me into seeing a doctor about my throat.

Our primary physician at the time was Dr. Robert Burns in Englewood, New Jersey. While a general practitioner he also had two specialties: internal medicine and pulmonary disorders. After a thorough physical examination he asked me to come back for pulmonary testing. That involved a number of tests, X-rays and the like. I had to blow through tubes that measured the pressure of both breathing in and out.

After that I was scheduled for another session to review the results.

On the appointed day I was ushered into Dr. Burns' office. I sat in the seat in front of his desk. Dr. Burns strode into the office with a folder in his left hand, turning pages with his right. Without a word he sat at his desk, examining the material. At last he pulled several sheets from the folder exclaiming, "Aha! Here we are!" He spread them out before him on his desk. Abruptly he looked up at me and said, "You're Robert Mitchell, aren't you?"

I nodded.

"Just checking." He smiled, almost embarrassed that he hadn't done so already. His finger followed the chart for a bit, then he picked up another paper and studied it. Suddenly laying them back down, he looked at me again with a more quizzical expression. He rubbed his chin and looked at the chart again. He slowly shook his head and looked up at me.

"Didn't you tell me you're an opera singer, or do I have the wrong person?"

"Oh yes, I sang opera all right. Over forty roles for nearly as many years."

"Really?" Again he seemed puzzled, and reexamined his chart and other papers.

"Well, either I have the wrong person, or – well, something isn't right..." he fidgeted.

"What do you mean? What's wrong?" I was beginning to get scared.

"You say you sang opera..."

"Yes. I don't understand..."

"This doesn't make sense. Your numbers and all indications here show that you have the lung capacity of a seventy year old man that smoked all his life. You couldn't possibly have sung opera. It doesn't make sense. Doesn't opera take enormous breath control?"

"Yes, but..."

"Well?" He glared at me as though I were lying.

"Yes, opera takes super-human breath control."

"Then, how in the world did you do it?"

"I don't know...exactly..." I paused, shrugged my shoulders, and held out my hands in a gesture of supplication. "But I did."

Suddenly my eyes were opened. No wonder I was always short of breath! Dr. Burns diagnosed me with chronic bronchial asthma. I had it all along. Singing kept it in check all those years, yet the disease cost me a major career. Many years prior during another physical, a different doctor noticed my enlarged diaphragm. He told me it was herniated. "Don't worry," he responded to my look of terror. "It's only cosmetic; nothing to be concerned about. Probably comes from pushing all those high notes through these constricted bronchial tubes, eh?" Chuckling, he pointed to my upper chest.

Little did he know…

As Filippo in Deceit Outwitted, a comic opera by Haydn

Opera Repertoire
Does not include musicals and chorus performances

Auber	FRA DIAVOLO	Lorenzo
Bellini	NORMA	Pollione
Bizet	CARMEN	Don Jose
Cimarosa	THE SECRET MARRIAGE	Paolino
Cornelius	BARBER OF BAGDAD	The Cadi
Donizetti	L'ELISIR D'AMORE	Nemorino
Floyd, Carlise	SUSANNAH	Sam
Gounod	FAUST	Faust
Haydn	DECEIT OUTWITTED	Filippo
Herbert	NAUGHTY MARIETTA	Dick Warrington
Lehar	THE MERRY WIDOW	Camille
Leoncavallo	I PAGLIACCI	Canio
Mascagni	CAVALLERIA RUSTICANA	Turiddu
Massenet	MANON	Des Grieux
	WERTHER	Werther
Menotti	AMAHL & THE NIGHT VISITORS	Kaspar
Mozart	ABDUCTION FROM THE SERAGLIO	Belmonte Pedrillo
	LA CLEMENZA DI TITO	Tito
	MAGIC FLUTE	Tamino First Priest
	DON GIOVANNI	Don Ottavio
Offenbach	TALES OF HOFFMANN	Hoffmann
Puccini	LA BOHEME	Rodolfo
	MADAMA BUTTERFLY	Pinkerton
Rimsky-Korsakov	SNOW MAIDEN	Tsar Berendey
Strauss	DIE FLEDERMAUS	Alfredo
Vaughan-Williams	MERRY WIVES OF WINSOR	Caius

Verdi	OBERTO	Riccardo
	I DUE FOSCARI	Jacopo Foscari
	RIGOLETTO	Duke of Mantua
	LA TRAVIATA	Alfredo
	IL TROVATORE	Manrico
	UN BALLO IN MASCHERA	Gustavo
	AIDA	Radames
	FALSTAFF	Fenton
Ward	CRUCIBLE	Rev. Parris

Amato Opera Company Repertoire

Bizet	CARMEN	Don Jose
Gounod	FAUST	Faust
Leoncavallo	I PAGLIACCI	Canio
Mascagni	CAVALLERIA RUSTICANA	Turiddu
Mozart	MAGIC FLUTE	Tamino
Offenbach	TALES OF HOFFMANN	Hoffmann
Puccini	LA BOHEME	Rodolfo
	MADAMA BUTTERFLY	Pinkerton
Verdi	OBERTO	Riccardo
	I DUE FOSCARI	Jacopo Foscari
	LA TRAVIATA	Alfredo
	IL TROVATORE	Manrico
	UN BALLO IN MASCHERA	Gustavo
	AIDA	Radames
	FALSTAFF	Fenton

Author Acknowledgements

How can I begin to thank the parade of teachers, coaches, conductors, and accompanists that shaped my singing career down through the years? My singer friend, James DeHaven, was the first to recognize me as a tenor. He insisted I go with him to New York to audition at the Mannes College of Music that fateful summer of 1960. Among my important teachers were Martial Singher, Olga Ryss, Emil Renan, Giovanni Consiglio, and Richard Fredericks. Coaches who shaped my repertoire were Igor Chichagov, Linda Hall, and Walter Taussig. Directors who guided me were Anthony Amato, Raymond Fowler, Joseph Bascetta, Michael Spierman, Carol Fox, and Alejandro Guzman. Two close colleagues that succumbed to AIDS were organist and coach Gerald Morton, and tenor Richard Schuller. Beula Silverman was the only person ever to write the Metropolitan Opera on my behalf.

On the writing side, the first person to redirect my writing style from academic to storytelling was Literary Agent, Deborah Carter. Among other very helpful ideas, she recommended I join a writing group. The BWG-Critters writers' group took me under their wing: Renee Ebert's unflagging support along with Rebecca Bartlett's precision edits and insights shaped me into the writer I am today. Thank you too, Donna, Steve, Walter and Jason.

Author Jaime Martinez-Tolentino was always there for me, and it was he who urged me to send my manuscript to ASJ Publishing.

Many thanks to the legion of good folks who cheered me on and stood by me through thick and thin, especially my loving wife Joan, and my sons, Rob and Randy.

Photo Credits

Bob as Hoffmann, left with Giulietta, right with Antonia (Amato Opera productions).

Bob as Eisenstein in studio shots of Die Fledermaus

Bob as Radames

Aida, Act 1, Triumphal Scene Amato Opera

Bob as Radames Aida, Act 1, "Celeste Aida" Amato Opera.

Bob as Faust, Prologue Amato Opera.   Bob as Faust, Garden Scene Amato Opera.

Regina Opera Presents 'I Pagliacci'

Page 21—BROOKLYN SPECTATOR—April 3, 1991

Canio, (Robert Mitchell), has just stabbed his unfaithful wife, Nedda, (Monica Ramirez-Geymayr) and her lover Silvio. (John Shelhart).

Canio, (Robert Mitchell), 'sings the famous aria, "Vesti la Giubba."

BY J. SAMRA SHIEPE

The Regina Opera Company presented Leoncavallo's "I Pagliacci" recently, as part of the company's 20th year celebration.

The fine assembly of participants resulted in a splendid production, keeping pace with the lofty standards of Brooklyn's premiere regional opera company, which its devoted audiences have learned to respect.

The title, "Pagliacci," is used to identify groups of Italian actors who roamed the remote countryside with their portable carts, entertaining their villagers with clowning, mimes and make-believe; using the popular play-within-a-play format, bringing joy and laughter wherever they went. However, Leoncavallo's inspiration was derived from a real-life tragic incident which he immortalized in this single operatic composition, with his stunning musical ability to reveal the clowns' garments were merely a facade to those agonizing emotions that lurked underneath.

When this reviewer was present, making his debut was tenor Robert Mitchell, cast in the title role. He gave a thrilling rendition of the great tenor aria, "Vesti La Giubba, Ridi Pagliaccio," registering the heart-rending agony of every brooding emotion dramatically, winning the admiration the enthusiastic audience. As his wife, Nedda, (and Columbine), soprano Monica Ramirez-Geymar, also making her debut, sang the beautiful, lilting Bellatella "Stridono lassu" which revealed her exquisite singing. Combined with her fine dramatic ability, she was a joy.

Baritone Eugene Green, as Tonio, also in love with the provocative Nedda, sang with his fine, round tones, the prologue; directing the audience more prohetically than he dreamed, a "slice of life" was about to un-

fold. The attractive baritone, John Shelhart, as Silvio, Nedda's lover, gave a most convincing performance, both vocally and dramatically. Tenor Martin Kugler sang the role of Beppe, another of Nedda's lovers.

On the whole, the dramatic, fictitious "play," was so skillfully enacted, that it gripped the audience with complete silence, before they let go with thunderous applause. The fine conductor, Gregory Ortega, is to be commended for enduring the unscheduled musical interruptions before finishing his interludes to the end, because of the enthusiasm of the audience.

The helpful villagers were Roman Henderson and Steve Reiss. The townspeople were represented by a score and more of Regina Opera's fine singers. The set design was by Richard Paratley; Selma Tepper and Terry Indiveri were the costume designers. Stage Director was Linda Cantoni.

THE BROOKLYN GRAPHIC WEEK JUNE 26-JULY 2, 1991

PAGE 17

Bellini's Norma Presented At Regina Opera

By Nino Pantano

Pictured L.-R. "Pollione, Robert Mitchell, "Oroveso" Michael Aihonte and "Norma" Phyllis Falletta.

Pictured L.-R. "Norma" Phyllis Falletta, "Adalgisa" Michelle Shayne and "Pollione" Robert Mitchell in Act II, Scene I where Norma has found out that her lover, Pollione, has been unfaithful to her. He has tried to convince Adalgisa to run away with him.

One of the most difficult roles in the soprano realm is that of "Norma" by the great Sicilian composer Vincenzo Bellini. Bellini (1805-1835) composed this tragic masterpiece in 1831 and it has been sung by such luminaries as Ponselle, Callas, Sutherland, Milanov and Caballe. The title role calls for a voice capable of florid singing and dramtic fervor as well. Norma is a role that is an awesome challenge and it cannot be treated lightly. The Metropolitan Opera occasionally revives it but only when it has a great soprano, a great mezzo-soprano, and a heroic tenor; regretably, Norma has not been presented at the Met for some time. It can kill!

When word got around that the Regina Opera Company was going to present Norma, the news was greeted with admiration plus justifiable skepticism. Those who love Bellini's music (he also composed La Sonnambula and I Puritani) would wish that justice be done to this beloved composer and master of mournful melody.

I am happy to report that the love triangle between the Druid Priestess, her Roman Proconsul, and the "other" woman (a virgin of the temple) was in splendid hands (and throats) the night of June 1.

Soprano Phyllis Falletta, the Norma of the evening, has a lyric coloratura voice, and when she first began to sing, one wondered whether she would be able to project her voice above the fortisimo orchestra when the time came. However, so secure is her technique, so intelligent her interpretation, so coordinated her interpretive gifts, that she proved herself to be an outstanding Norma. Her first act aria "Casta diva" in which she prays for peace to the goddess of the moon, was sung with lovely fluidity, pure sweet tones, perfect fioritura, and a stunning accent at the finale that earned her an ovation.

Her roman warrior lover, Pollione, was heroically sung by tenor Robert Mitchell. Indeed, his act one aria "Meco all' altar di Venere" was a tour de force. His is a solid voice, dramatic, but also able to sing sweetly when called upon to do so. When confronted by Norman, who has secretly loved him and has borne him two children, and by his new love, the young virgin priestess Adalgisa, he looked like a boy who got caught with his hand in the cookie jar (or two cookie jars, in this instance). However, his humble demeanor quickly changes when he tries to force Adalgisa to go with him. Norma is furious with Pollione but forging to the innocent Adalgisa.

Adalgisa as portrayed by Michelle Shayne was every bit a match for Norma. Ms. Shayne is blessed with an impressive mezzo-soprano voice capable of flooding the house with volume and soaring above the orchestra. Yet her second act duel with Norma. "Mira, o Norma" was sung in perfect harmony and the two voices sang this incredible duet with stunning results. Ms. Shayne

has youthful ardor and this stood in good contrast with Norma's more sophisticated and worldly demeanor.

When Norman discovers Pollione's treachery, she first feels that she must kill their two out-of-wedlock children, reminders of the vow of chastity she has broken. Norma cannot take their lives and asks Adalgisa to care for them. The scene with Norma and Adalgisa caressing the children was very touching and youngster Susann Fink and Carrie Vasquez were never restless and did a splendid job as the tragedy surrounded them. Norma's friend and confidante, Clotilde, who helps Norma care for the children, was pleasingly played by Diane Oegina.

The second act has much exciting music aside from "Mira, o Norma." Oroveso, the Archdruid, asks Norma to name the sacrifical victim who has broken her sacred vows and betrayed her land. Although Norma tells Pollione that

she will denounce Adalgisa, but she recants and names herself. A repentent Pollione decides to join her in death and Norma convinces Oroveso to take care of the children. Michael Aihone, sang Oroveso in a warm bass voice that was richer at the bottom than on top. When Norma and Pollione mount the pyre in the last scene, it is one of the most thrilling finales in all opera. The Regina Opera audience rewarded the entire ensemble with well deserved cheers and bravos. All the performers were cheered, including the talented tenor Kenneth Jaffe, who was Flavio, aide-de-camp to Pollione.

The stage director Pauline Kent Dennis did a superb job. The sets and costumes were evocative of the era and the program listed special thanks to Evelyn Quaife for her scholarship on Druid rituals which was of great value in the moonlit "Casta diva" scene in

which Norma distributes the sacred mistletoe.

The Regina Opera is blessed with one of the finest orchestras as led by Maestro Guzmaan. The instrumentalists and chorus thrilled and excited us from thhe overture to the finale, including the choral exaltations to war complete with the powerful gong. If one might criticize a rose for its thorns, some of the orchestral fortissimos were a bit trying to those singers not blessed with stentorian equipment, although the score is so exciting that one perhaps has a problem putting the "brakes" on the orchestra. Nonetheless, the Norma of thie evening, Phyllis Falletta's 'bel canto' technique allowed her voice to soar to the heavens and this Norma performance by the incomparable Regina Opera had us all heavenbound. Congratulations to Brooklyn's greatest resident company, the Regina Opera, for this superb production.

About The Author

Long before the Rev. Robert P. Mitchell was a "reverend," he sang opera for over forty years. He appeared in fifteen productions with New York's Amato Opera Company alone, and in numerous productions with fourteen other "minor league" companies in the NY-NJ metropolitan area. His most prestigious appearance occurred on Saturday, January 31, 1987 as Pinkerton in Madama Butterfly with Opera Classics of New Jersey at the Orrie de Nooyer Auditorium in Hackensack, New Jersey, with Maestro Anton Coppola conducting. The author was the only non-Metropolitan Opera or non-New York City Opera singer in the cast. That performance led to singing with the late Maestro Alfredo Silipini, then Artistic Director of the New Jersey State Opera.

Rev. Mitchell was born in 1939 in the small village of McVeytown, in south central Pennsylvania. By the time he was ready for school, the Mitchell family had moved to the north central Pennsylvania town of Lock Haven. He grew up there, graduated with honors, and attended both Lock Haven State Teachers College and Mansfield STC before he went to New York City to begin serious operatic studies at the Mannes College of Music. On the day he registered, he met his future wife, who happened to be on the other side of the registration desk. They married in 1962. In 2012 they celebrated their fiftieth wedding anniversary. They have two sons and three grandchildren, and now live in the scenic Delaware Water Gap region of northeastern Pennsylvania.

In addition to his singing career, Rev. Mitchell worked for The New York State Employment Service, the T. J. Lipton Company, and Scholastic, Inc., the New York-based educational publisher. From 1968 to 1998 he enjoyed a career with Scholastic as a manger, first in the Personnel Department, and later in Marketing Systems Management. Alongside his Scholastic career, he performed full productions of more than thirty opera roles and some musicals, sang each weekend in churches and synagogues, and sang concerts in numerous venues, as well as on WQXR and WGN radio stations.

The author holds a B.S. degree in Voice and Opera from the Mannes College of Music, and a Master of Divinity degree from the New

Brunswick (NJ) Theological Seminary. He and his wife co-pastored a church in the Hudson Valley for seven years following his retirement from Scholastic. He holds certificates in Direct Marketing from New York University, and is a Certified Interim Minister. He currently serves as Pastor of the Pleasant Valley Presbyterian Church in Brodheadsville, PA.

Bob has taught philosophy at Marist College in Poughkeepsie, NY and as a substitute teacher in the local East Stroudsburg School District.

He is a member of the national Phi Mu Alpha Music Fraternity.

Made in the USA
Lexington, KY
03 October 2014